THEY CALLED THEM GREASERS

They Called Them Greasers,
ANGLO ATTITUDES TOWARD MEXICANS IN TEXAS, 1821–1900

by Arnoldo De León

 University of Texas Press, Austin

Requests for permission to reproduce material
from this work should be sent to:
    Permissions
    University of Texas Press
    Box 7819
    Austin, Texas 78713-7819

Publication of this work has been made possible in part
by a grant from the Andrew W. Mellon Foundation.

LIBRARY OF CONGRESS CATALOGING IN PUBLICATION DATA
De León, Arnoldo, 1945–
    They called them greasers.
    Bibliography: p.
    Includes index.
    1. Mexican Americans—Texas—Public opinion—History—
19th century. 2. Public opinion—Texas—History—19th
century. 3. Texas—Race relations. I. Title.
F395.M5D43 1983 976.4'0046872 82-24850
ISBN 0-292-78054-0 (pbk.)

♾ The paper used in this publication meets the minimum
requirements of American National Standard for Information
Sciences—Permanence of Paper for Printed Library Materials,
ANSI Z39.48-1984.

to my wife DOLORES
and my daughters PAULINE and JESSICA

Contents

The Tejano Community. From Arnoldo De León, *The Tejano Community, 1836–1900*. Reproduced by permission of the University of New Mexico Press.

Preface

From the moment they landed on the American continent, white people in their role as discoverers, settlers, pioneers, and landholders manifested unique feelings toward the colored or *mestizo* (mixed-blood) people they encountered. This study deals with only one specific aspect of those feelings—how whites felt about Mexicans in the state of Texas in the nineteenth century. It seeks to ascertain what beliefs whites held, to discover the genesis and roots of those attitudes, to demonstrate in what ways and methods they were expressed, and how they became a sanctioned, functional, and institutionalized part of white society in the attempted debasement of Texas-Mexicans.

Specifically, the book focuses on those feelings as a history of attitudes. It centers on Anglo perceptions of Mexicans in only one state of the Union and does not attempt to make a comparison with the ways whites imagined or dealt with other peoples of color. Nor does it place the study of attitudes within the total structure of United States history or of the state or nation's political, social, and economic institutions. But I believe that a study of those attitudes in isolation merits a monograph; thus, this is an effort to sharpen the focus on white feelings toward Mexicanos that are found in the works of other students of Mexican American history.[1]

In its interpretation, the monograph depicts the nuances of the white mind rather unpleasantly. It also points to the fact that those who have traditionally dominated Texas history have published works that reveal, in fact and interpretation, serious flaws, deficiencies of research, and detectable bias, especially concerning the relationships between whites and Mexicans. Strongly influenced by Eugene C. Barker, Walter Prescott Webb, and Rupert N. Richardson, other historians have uncritically followed their mentors' paths, overlooking a long racist and ethnocentric tradition toward blacks and Indians that was transposed upon native Texas *castas* as a matter of course. These same historians also failed to comment upon an austere Anglo-American moral code that translated the morality of Mexicanos into a "defective" one; a chauvinistic sentiment that discriminated against "un-American" nonconformists; and the fact that Texas society placed few social restrictions on a long tradition of violence which ultimately aided and abetted white Texans in keeping ethnic minorities subordinated.

The conclusions presented here are set forth in the hope they will prove to be thought-provoking, rather than controversial. To me, these ideas are valid points of departure for a complete and necessary re-evaluation of many aspects of Texas history, especially as it relates to nonwhite cultures in the state. White Texans have left an enormous record expressly related to their attitudes toward Mexicans. True, there are no discourses akin to Thomas Jefferson's reflections on blacks in his *Notes on the State of Virginia*, but the evidence abounds in observations, expressions, actions, and comments of whites as itinerants, observers, pioneers, immigrants, and citizens. Whites did record their impressions of Mexicans, an indication of how very present the Mexicans were in their minds. And they expressed their opinions in a candidly biased tone. The truth of the matter is that whites saw very few redemptive attributes in Tejanos; and aside from patronizing compliments about hospitality, courtesy, and other amenities, their remarks and opinions tended toward disparagement.

Anglos recorded their strongest impulses during those historical moments when they made contact with concentrated pockets of Tejanos—in Central Texas from the 1830s to the 1850s and in South Texas at mid-century. Travelers and incoming settlers left a lengthy record of precisely how they felt about Mexicans in those two regions. The way they felt determined both the subtle and the violent aspects of race relations in the antebellum period.

The Civil War proved a dividing mark. The state entered a lull in the 1860s, and, by the time that things resumed their regular gait after Reconstruction, circumstances were no longer the same: contact between whites and Mexicans was more common (except in West Texas) and white relations with Native Americans and blacks took a different turn as the Indians were finally subdued and slavery abolished. Furthermore, the state in general passed into a new epoch. By then the early perceptions were so entrenched among permanent residents as part of institutionalized attitudes, that Texans when recording old feelings of race and ethnocentrism no longer expressed them as strongly as they had when they were newcomers. Exceptions were travelers and more recent arrivals to the state, latecomers searching for opportunity in burgeoning South Texas, and migrants into developing West Texas in the 1870s and 1880s who were encountering Mexicans for the first time and took notice of what older Texans had observed before the Civil War. It was they who now expressed the more exaggerated responses when noting things that local whites considered "matter-of-fact" or "natural." The native population by this time accepted Mexicanos in the patterns they had forged during the initial encounters and treated them accordingly. These feelings that "Mexicans were like that" remained the rationalization for the Anglo citizens of Texas who continued discriminatory and violent actions against Mexicanos.

In formulating my argument, I have remained receptive to the idea that the expressions of whites toward Mexicans were partially ones of ethnocentrism. However, I cannot help but support the theory that whites in the nineteenth century were more racists than cultural chauvinists. The evidence is heavy that Anglos perceived the physical contrasts of Mexicans as indicating mental and temperamental weaknesses. Moreover, my findings square with recent scholarship which argues that racism originated either in the Western psyche, in capitalist social development, or in religion, and that native peoples in the path of white civilization have historically been either exterminated or reduced to a hereditary caste because of the peculiar strain of that racism.[2] In any case, this is a study of both Anglo ethnocentrism and racist attitudes toward Mexicans.

Only in passing have I attempted to take issue with the several stereotypes advanced by Anglos. Certainly, some of what white men said about Mexicans was true; but most was not. The Tejano community that Anglos observed was more a product of their attitudes than a correct perception of that society. It has not been my purpose to counter the statements of Anglos with lengthy descriptions of what the Tejano community was actually like. My intention here is solely to interpret Anglo attitudes toward Tejanos. Those wishing a more correct portrayal of Texas Mexican society may turn to my earlier book, *The Tejano Community, 1836–1900.*

Finally, several pathbreaking and significant books spurred initially by the civil rights movements of recent decades influenced my thinking about Anglo feelings toward Mexicanos. Like other writers on white attitudes toward Afro-Americans, Native Americans, or Mexican Americans, I immediately acknowledge my debt to Winthrop D. Jordan's *White over Black: American Attitudes toward the*

Negro, 1550–1812. But other works written since then (too numerous to mention) have also been models to emulate, and I have learned much from them. Happily, some of those studies are paying long-due attention to Chicanos, among them Ronald T. Takaki's *Iron Cages: Race and Culture in Nineteenth Century America* and Reginald Horsman's *Race and Manifest Destiny: The Origins of American Racial Anglo-Saxonism.* This book is a contribution to that current interest.

My thanks go to the people at Angelo State University's Porter Henderson Library, who have cheerfully assisted me throughout the years in my research efforts, and to the members of the History Department at the same institution, who have ever granted me their encouragement. Professor Malcolm D. McLean, of the University of Texas at Arlington, dutifully made editorial corrections as he has done in so many of my other works. David J. Weber of Southern Methodist University and Ricardo Romo of the University of Texas at Austin made useful suggestions for revising the manuscript. Particularly valuable in this regard was an insightful and candid critique by my good friend Barry A. Crouch of Gallaudet College, reminding me of my responsibility to present the research in a calm and objective manner. The final product is all the better for the contribution of these scholars.

Jo White typed the manuscript, and I am indebted to her for that.

A Note on Terminology

A number of different labels have been used over the years to distinguish the various ethnic groups living in Texas. In this book, such expressions are used according to the following definitions:

Anglo: any white, English-speaking, non-Mexican American.
casta: a person of mixed Spanish, Indian, and African ancestry.
creole: English form of *criollo*.
criollo: a person of Spanish ancestry born in the New World.
Isleña: female descendant of any of several families that came to
San Antonio from the Canary Islands in 1731.
mestizo: a person of mixed Spanish and Indian ancestry.
Mexican: a person from Mexico, or a person of Mexican ancestry.
(No attempt is made to distinguish Mexican citizens, Mexican
immigrants to Texas, and Texan or American citizens of Mexican ancestry.)
Mexicana: a Mexican or Mexican American woman.
Mexicano: used interchangeably with *Mexican*.
pelado: a contemptuous term used by Anglos in reference to what
they considered the lowest class of Mexicans.
peninsular: Spaniard (from the Iberian Peninsula).
Tejana: feminine form of *Tejano*.
Tejano: a Mexican resident of Texas, whether born in Mexico or
the United States (or Republic of Texas).
Texan: an Anglo resident of Texas.
Texian: term of self-reference used by Anglos during the early years
of residence in Texas.

There is a report in camp that our company has been ordered to Corpus Christi which I hope is so. I am getting rather tired of the Rio Grande and the *greasers*, of all the contemptable, despecable people on Earth the greasers in my estimation are the lowest, meaner even than the Cummanche. They are ugly, theiving, rascally in every way and to be educated only makes a greaser the grander rascal. I think the whole nation ought to be peoned rich and poor, they would make the best plantation hands in the world. They fear and respect authority and are a great deal moore humble and less inteligent than our negroes.

(Letter of George L. Robertson to his sister,
from Rancho Palmito, March 26, 1864;
George L. Robertson Papers, 1839–1869,
University of Texas Archives, Austin)

1. Initial Contacts: Redeeming Texas from Mexicans, 1821–1836

Most whites who first met Tejanos in the 1820s had never had prior experiences with Mexicans nor encountered them anywhere else. Yet their reaction to them upon contact was contemptuous, many thinking Mexicans abhorrent. What caused pioneers to feel this way? Why were their attitudes bigoted instead of neutral? What did they find in Mexicans that aroused xenophobic behavior, or what was it within themselves that generated that response?

According to one Texas historian, Anglo settlers who entered Texas accepted Mexicans on a basis of equality initially and did not react scornfully toward the native Tejanos until the Texas war for independence of 1836. Relationships before then, according to him, were characterized by a marked tolerance, lack of basic antipathy between the two races, and an almost total lack of friction traceable to racial problems.[1] In the opinion of another student of Anglo attitudes during the period 1821–1845, white feelings toward Mexicans were very complex, at times contradictory, and constantly in flux.[2]

The latest scholarship on the subject of racial and cultural attitudes, however, does not sustain these arguments. Americans moving to the west, recent studies indicate, had much more in mind than settling the land and creating prosperous communities. Cultural heirs to Elizabethans and Puritans, those moving into hinterlands sensed an "errand into the wilderness" and felt a compelling need to control all that was beastly—sexuality, vice, nature, and colored peoples. Order and discipline had to be rescued from the wilds in the name of civilization and Christianity. Moving westward with this mission uppermost in their minds, whites psychologically needed to subdue the external world—forests, beasts, and other peoples—for the rational had to be ever in command. Coming into constant encounter with peoples of color in wilderness settings, these sensitive whites struggled against noncivilization. To allow an inverse order and a concomitant surrender of themselves and their liberties to primitive things was to allow chaos to continue when God's will was to impose Christian order.[3]

The desire to bring fields and Indians under submission did not emanate solely from religious passion but was also a product of the individual compulsion to repress instinctual urges. Within humanity were encased base impulses (e.g., sexuality, savagery) that were just as primitive and animalistic as the things of the forest which demanded domination. Killing, destruction, subordination, and appropriation of lands not only brought the external wilderness under control but also served as a form of release for the animal within. In prevailing over primitive things through violence, whites found regeneration, but their efforts also resulted in the uglier manifestations of racism.[4] Therein lay the seed for the perverse responses toward Mexicanos in the first encounter.[5]

Waves of Anglo settlers first entered Texas when the Mexican government in 1821 granted colonization rights in the province to a Missouri entrepreneur named Moses Austin. Hundreds more followed thereafter, coming to Mexican Texas under the aegis of Moses' son, Stephen, and other empresarios. Most were not radically different from the pre–nineteenth-century pioneers. Like them, they entertained a strong belief in themselves and the superiority of their way of life.

Why, asked the historian Samuel M. Lowrie in his study of culture conflict in Texas, were Americans as narrow and freedom loving as frontiersmen willing to settle in a country as religiously intolerant and undemocratic as Mexico?[6] Perhaps because they felt it their duty to make order of what they perceived as chaos. Certainly they uttered such sentiments many times, though Lowrie did not discern it, given the state of scholarship in the 1930s when he wrote his study. As William H. Wharton, one of the more radical agitators for independence from Mexico, put it in an appeal for American support as the revolution went on in Texas,

> The justice and benevolence of God, will forbid that the delightful region of Texas should again become a howling wilderness, trod only by savages, or that it should be permanently benighted by the ignorance and superstition, the anarchy and rapine of Mexican misrule. The Anglo-American race are destined to be for ever the proprietors of this land of *promise* and *fulfilment. Their* laws will govern it, *their* learning will enlighten it, their enterprise will improve it. *Their* flocks will

range its boundless pastures, for *them* its fertile lands will yield their luxuriant harvests: its beauteous rivers will waft the products of *their* industry and enterprise, and *their* latest posterity will here enjoy legacies of "price unspeakable," in the possession of homes fortified by the genius of liberty, and sanctified by the spirit of a beneficent and tolerant religion. This is inevitable, for the wilderness of Texas has been redeemed by Anglo-American blood and enterprise. The colonists have carried with them the language, the habits, and the lofty love of liberty, that has always characterized and distinguished their ancestors. They have identified them indissolubly with the country.[7]

But none was more articulate than Stephen F. Austin, who several times before the war for independence confessed, almost stereotypically, that his intent was "to redeem Texas from the wilderness." In one of his most eloquent expressions, he averred: "My object, the sole and only desire of my ambitions since I first saw Texas, was to redeem it from the wilderness—to settle it with an intelligent honorable and interprising [*sic*] people."[8]

To Austin, redemption could come by "whitening" Texas—or, phrased differently, by making it a cultural and racial copy of the United States. In August 1835, he wrote that the best interests of the nation required "that Texas should be effectually, and fully, Americanized—that is—settled by a population that will harmonize with their neighbors on the *East*, in language, political principles, common origin, sympathy, and even interest." It was well known, he continued, that his object had always been to fill up Texas with a North American population. "I wish a great immigration from Kentucky, Tennessee, *every where*, passports, or no passports, *any how*. For fourteen years I have had a hard time of it, but nothing shall daunt my courage or abate my exertions to complete the main object of my labors—to *Americanize Texas*. This fall, and winter, will fix our fate—a great immigration will settle the question."[9]

At the national level, Americans had never been oblivious to the prospects of rescuing Texas from its alleged primitive status. At all times, there had been those in Washington who had similar thoughts and expressed them publicly. Among them was Henry Clay, who asked in 1821: "By what race should Texas be peopled?" Lest it be settled by others who would make it a "place of despotism and slaves, of the Inquisition and superstition," it should be taken over by settlers from the United States who would transplant to it the free institutions of Anglo-Americans. Should Texas then break off from the United States for some reason, Clay affirmed, at least it would have been rescued from a race alien to everything that Americans held dear.[10]

Clay did not stop at rhetoric. While he was Secretary of State, he and President John Quincy Adams instructed Joel R. Poinsett, the United States Minister to Mexico, to attempt to purchase Texas. Mexico, which had never put Texas up for sale, squarely rejected the proposal, only to see it repeated. When Andrew Jackson assumed office in 1829, he urged Poinsett to renew his efforts, authorizing the minister to offer $5 million for whatever amount of Texas Mexico would surrender. Similar futile attempts at negotiating the purchase of Texas continued until the time of the revolution.[11]

What whites refused to accept was a state of affairs in which chaos presided over them. But what exactly was it that they considered as disorder? Texas was already settled and under the rule of a government, heir to centuries of Spanish civilization. Something else disturbed them, for to them, a connection existed in the new land between the state of civilization and chaos. Thus all the discussion about rescuing Texas from primitivism. The newcomers saw the Tejanos as mongrels, uncivilized, and un-Christian—a part of the wilderness that must be subdued. Living in Mexico and Texas were a sort of people who threatened the march of white civilization.

Incontrovertibly, as far as whites were concerned, order and discipline were missing. For Anglo settlers who arrived in Texas imported certain ideas from the United States, which regarded the native Mexican population as less than civilized. These attitudes ranged from xenophobia against Catholics and Spaniards to racial prejudice against Indians and blacks. Thus Mexicanos were doubly suspect, as heirs to Catholicism and as descendants of Spaniards, Indians, and Africans.

In England, hostile feelings toward the Roman Church originated in the sixteenth century with Henry VIII's religious and political break with the Pope and were hardened by conflict with Catholic Spain. The English mind readily thought in terms of a Catholic-Spanish alliance, conjured by Satan himself, from which nothing less than demonic designs could be expected. Additionally, the English associated the Spanish with cruelty and brutality. Alleged Spanish tyranny in the Netherlands during the latter half of the sixteenth century as well as atrocities toward the Indians in Latin America produced an image of the Spaniard as heartless and genocidal. And, finally, the English saw the Spanish as an embodiment of racial impurity. For hundreds of years, racial mixing or *mestizaje* had occurred in the Iberian peninsula between Spaniards and Moors. At a time when Elizabethans were becoming more and more sensitive to the significance of color—equating whiteness with purity and Christianity and blackness with baseness and the devil—Spaniards came to be thought of as not much better than light-skinned Moors and Africans.

English immigrants to the North American colonies probably brought those ideas with them and were certainly exposed to them through anti-Catholic and anti-Spanish literature constantly arriving in the new society. Men of letters, ministers, and propagandists helped in disseminating such notions. Military clashes along the Georgia-Florida border in the eighteenth century only intensified the hatred.

As for the Mexican aborigines, the English conceived of them as degenerate creatures—un-Christian, uncivilized, and racially impure. From letters, histories, and travel narratives, English writers put together a portrait that turned the people of Mexico into a degraded humanity. The natives subscribed to heathenism, and witches and other devilish agents permeated their culture. They partook of unholy things like polygamy, sodomy, and incest and rejected Christianity outright. Furthermore, they practiced savage rituals like human sacrifice and cannibalism. Of all the Latin American inhabitants, the Mexican Indians seemed the most beastly, for though they were in many ways the most advanced of all the New World peoples, they exercised the grossest violation of civility by these practices. Stories of Aztec gods like Quetzalcoatl who were half man and half beast and accounts of exotic Aztec rites only convinced the English of the Indians' place on the fringes of humankind, with dubious claims to existence, civilization, and Christian salvation.

While such images of the Mexican natives may not have been as widespread as those held of Spaniards, they were nonetheless familiar to many colonists. In newspapers, recent histories, and re-editions of old propaganda materials, furthermore, colonists were able to read things about the origins of the Mexicans which perpetuated enriched images acquired from the mother country.[12]

In addition to ideas that had been fashioned vicariously, there were those that arose from intimate contact with other peoples whom whites esteemed no more than the Mexican aborigines or the Spaniards. The long history of hostilities against North American Indians on the frontier and the institution of Afro-American slavery molded negative attitudes toward dark skin, "savagery," "vice," and interracial sex. The majority of those who responded to empresario calls most assuredly thought along those lines, for they came from the states west of the Appalachians and south of the Ohio River— Louisiana, Alabama, Arkansas, Tennessee, Missouri, Mississippi, Georgia, and Kentucky. A significant number were Eastern born, but had been part of the frontier movement before their transplantation into Texas.[13] From the Southern and frontier-oriented culture they had acquired a certain repulsion for dark-skinned people and a distaste for miscegenation. Believing that the mores of their own provincial institutions should apply in the new frontier, they assumed a posture of superiority and condescension toward the natives. By conditioning, they were predisposed to react intolerantly to people they found different from themselves but similar to those they considered as enemies and as inferiors. Along with dislike for Spaniards and the Indians of Latin America, these perceptions produced a mode of thinking that set the contours of the primordial response.

And what particularly provoked this reaction? Most Tejanos were descendants of Tlascalan Indians and *mestizo* soldiers from Coahuila. Additionally, a few in Nacogdoches were the offspring of people from Louisiana and reflected that area's racial amalgam, including Indians and blacks. Throughout the province, Tejanos had intermarried among themselves and with Christianized Indian women from local missions so that the colonists continued as a mixed-blood population.[14] Their contrast to "white" and salient kindred to "black" and "red" made Mexicans subject to treatment commensurate with the odious connotations whites attached to colors, races, and cultures dissimilar to their own.

Manifestly, Americans who immigrated to Texas confronted the native Mexicans with certain preconceptions about their character. Whites believed that the inhabitants of the province had descended from a tradition of paganism, depravity, and primitivism. Mexicans were a type of folk that Americans should avoid becoming.

The fact of the matter was that whites had little contact with Tejanos up to 1836, for most of the Mexican population was concentrated in the San Antonio and La Bahía areas, quite a distance from the Anglo colonies. But whites knew what they would find in Texas before contact confirmed their convictions. They encountered biologically decadent and inferior people because their thoughts had been shaped by the aforementioned circumstances. Thus, Mexicans lived in ways that Anglos equated with an opprobrious condition. They inhabited primitive shelters. William F. Gray, a land agent

from Virginia, comparing Mexicans with the black American culture he knew, pronounced some of the Mexican homes "miserable
shabby *jacales*" scarcely equal in appearance to the Afro-American
houses in the suburbs of his state.[15] Mexicans adhered to a different
religion: they were completely the "slaves of Popish superstitions
and despotism" and religion was understood not as an affection of
the heart and soul but as one requiring personal mortification in
such superficialities as penances and other rituals.[16] If Anglos and
Mexicans were not inherently different peoples, editorialized the
Texian and Emigrant's Guide in 1835, habit, education, and religion
had made them essentially so.[17]

Additionally, Texians thought that Mexicans' cultural habits
clashed with American values, such as the work ethic. Mexicanos
appeared a traditional, backward aggregate, an irresponsibly passive
people dedicated to the present and resigned not to probe the uni-
verse about them. An American arriving in Nacogdoches in 1833
found the citizens there the most "lazy indolent poor Starved set of
people as ever the Sun Shined upon." He could not comprehend
their lethargy by day, nor their inclination to play the violin and
dance the entire night.[18] J. C. Clopper of Ohio reasoned in 1828 that
Mexicanos were "too ignorant and indolent for enterprises and too
poor and *dependent* were they otherwise capacitated."[19] Mexicanos
habitually succumbed to indolence and ease and indulged themselves in smoking, music, dancing, horse-racing, and other sports,
noted David Woodman, a promoter for a New York and Boston land
company, while activity, industry, and frugality marched on in the
new American settlements.[20] "The vigor of the descendents of the
sturdy north will never mix with the phlegm of the indolent Mexicans," Sam Houston (the future hero of the war for independence)
argued in January 1835 in an address to the citizens of Texas, "no
matter how long we may live among them."[21] In contrast to the newcomers, Tejanos were chained by custom to complacency, and instead of committing themselves to progress, they preferred fun
and frolic. Some three years after Mexico opened Texas to Anglo-
American settlement, Anthony R. Clark complained that Spaniards
in the District of Nacogdoches, "generally of the lower sort and illit-
terate [sic]," would rather "spend days in gambling to gain a few bits
than to make a living by honest industry."[22] William B. Dewees, who
lived in San Antonio in the late 1820s, found Bexareños totally
hedonistic. "Their whole study seems to be for enjoyment. Mirth
and amusement occupy their whole time. If one is fond of balls and
theatres, he can here have an opportunity of attending one every eve-

ning. Almost every species of dissipation is indulged in, except drinking."[23] In Goliad, the Mexicans had such a strong predisposition for gaming that almost all the inhabitants in 1833 were gamblers and smugglers, said empresario Dr. John Charles Beales.[24] And Alexander McCrae, touring Texas in 1835 under the auspices of the Wilmington Emigrating Society, remarked in astonishment: "I for the first time saw females betting at a public gambling table; I do not suppose they were of respectable standing in society, from the company they kept; but I am told that it is not all uncommon for Mexican *ladies* to be seen gambling in public."[25]

Acting further to stimulate negative attitudes was the racial composition of Tejanos, who, in the white mind, were closely identified with other colored peoples. For two hundred years, ideas that black men lusted for white women and notions that slaves were of a heathen or "savage" condition had played upon Americans' fantasies; the result had been the institutional debasement of blacks because of their race. Images of the Indian as fierce, hostile, and barbaric similarly affixed themselves in the thoughts of white settlers, and the constant confrontation over land led more to the reaffirmation of these images than to their dissolution. Consequently, when whites arrived in Texas, they unconsciously transferred onto the new "colored" folk they encountered a pseudo-scientific lore acquired from generations of interaction with blacks and Indians.

Travelers, who frequently came in contact with Tejanos, plainly discerned the Mexicans' relation to the black and red peoples. At no time did Americans hold up Frenchmen, or Germans, or themselves for that matter, as a people who physically resembled Mexicans—comparison invariably was with Indians and blacks. Several factors steered discussion in that direction: Anglos were not about to elevate Mexicans to the level of European whiteness; their own sense of superiority turned Tejanos into a people lesser than themselves; and obviously, in any comparison, Mexicans were going to resemble their progenitors. Thus, whites often likened Mexicans to Africans and Native Americans. When Clopper mentioned the complexion of the Tejanos, he thought it "a shade brighter than that of the aborigines of the country."[26] On the other hand, the land agent Gray stamped Tejanos as a "swarthy looking people much resembling our mulattos, some of them nearly black."[27] Sam Houston asked his compatriots (in the aforementioned address) if they "would bow under the yoke of these half-Indians,"[28] while abolitionist Benjamin Lundy, in Laredo in 1834, remarked that the Mexicans in the town looked like mulattoes.[29] Even when commentators omitted drawing comparisons about color, they nonetheless made reference to the Mexicans' dark complexion. One traveler asserted that because of it they were "readily designated at first sight."[30] The same association with Indians and Africans was also apparent in caustic comments about the Mexicans' ancestors. A Texan identifying himself as "H. H." in a letter to the *New Orleans Bee* in 1834 pronounced the people of Mexico the most "degraded and vile; the unfortunate race of Spaniard, Indian and African, is so blended that the worst qualities of each predominate."[31] Two years later, when the Texans were locked in a fateful struggle with the Mexican nation, leaders of the rebellion appealed to their comrades by reminding them that Mexicans were "the adulterate and degenerate brood of the once high-spirited Castilian."[32]

In addition to all their other discoveries about Mexicans, whites in the period between 1821 and 1836 thought Tejanos lax in virtue. A number of aspects of Mexican morality bothered them, including the native *fandango*, a dance of a sinuous sort with sexually suggestive moves. George W. Smyth from Tennessee witnessed it in Nacogdoches upon his arrival in 1830, and was surprised "that the priest and all participated, so contrary to all my pre-conceived notions of propriety."[33] Asahel Langworthy, a New York lawyer and land speculator, found the dance somewhat uncivilized, identifying it with lack of culture and refinement. "I witnessed one afternoon," he wrote, "a Spanish *fandango* danced in the open air by a party of these people, evidently of a low class."[34]

Because of the apparent revelry of such recreational forms, whites began early on to assume Mexicans had a defective morality, and Mexican attitudes toward sexuality strengthened the white image of Mexicans as sensuous and voluptuous. Despite the close supervision given unmarried girls to prevent intercourse with their male counterparts, Clopper alleged, "soon as married they are scarcely the same creatures—giving the freest indulgence to their naturally gay and enthusiastic dispositions, as if liberated from all moral restraints."[35] To the Ohioan, Mexicans were not cut from the same moral fabric as Americans.

But even if Mexicans as a race were sexually degenerate, some exception might be made for the females, especially by those men wandering into areas like Béxar where white women were scarce, and thus where Mexican women might be attractive, even if they were of mixed blood. Among those venturing into San Antonio at this early date was Clopper, who considered the local women handsome of person and regular in feature, with black, sparkling eyes and "a brighter hue" than the men.[36] Like others of this era, he had a preference for those who came close to the American ideal of female beauty and purity. Becoming friendly with one of the Castilian *señoritas*, Clopper wrote a meticulous description of his acquaintance. "She was of the middle size, her person of the finest symmetry," he noted, "moving through the mazes of the *fandango* with all the graces that distinguished superiority of person of mind and of soul. Her features were beautiful forming in their combination an expression that fixed the eye of the observer as with a spell, her complexion was of the loveliest, the snowy brightness of her well turned forehead beautifully contrasting with the carnation tints of her cheeks. A succession of smiles were continually sporting around her mouth," he elaborated, "her pouting cherry lips were irresistible and even when closed seemed to have utterance—her eye—but I have no such language as seemed to be spoken by it else might I tell how dangerous was it to meet its lustre and feel its quick thrilling scrutiny of the heart as tho' the very fire of its expression was conveyed with its beamings." The admirer admitted in closing: "I felt lonely and sad as a stranger in that place and a vision so lovely coming so unexpectedly before me could not fail to awaken tender recollections and altogether make an impression not to be forgotten."[37]

Though not much else was said on the issue of interracial sex, at least one Texan brought up a theme that would preoccupy white males after 1836. Mexican women, he thought, manifested a "decided preference" for foreigners, and would willingly consent to marriage should they be approached. "Where a Mexican woman becomes attached there are few who can love more warmly," he added.[38] And it would probably be safe to conjecture that at least some of those women that the future hero of the Alamo, William Barrett Travis, "*chingó*," were Mexicans.[39]

Despite their comments about passionate Mexican women, whites did not say much about sexually virile males. During the revolution, however, hysterical Texians did inject a sexual dimension into the war—crying out that Mexican soldiers were sexual threats to white women. "What can be expected for the *fair Daughters* of chaste *white women* when their own country women are prostituted, by a licensed soldiery, as an inducement to push forward into the Colonies, where they may find fairer game!" feared James W. Fannin, who later was killed in the Goliad massacre.[40] John W. Hall, a spirited mover of independence, asked the public to imagine what would happen if Mexican soldiers gained a foothold in Texas soil? Beloved wives, mothers, daughters, sisters, and helpless innocent children would be given up to the dire pollution and massacre of the barbarians, he claimed.[41] And from the Alamo, Travis also raised the spectre of "the pollution of [the Texans'] wives and daughters" by the Mexican soldiers of General Antonio López de Santa Anna.[42]

The vision of Mexican rapists seemingly reflected white men's state of mind as of 1836. Probably, they saw in Mexicans the same threat that horrified them in black males, and it was too early then for them to have formulated other perceptions. As it turned out, no violations were reported and the rape theme practically disappeared, rarely to crop up again, even though in subsequent times Texans faced other threats of Mexican violence. After the episode, Anglos seldom saw Mexicans as a danger to white women.

The events of 1836 brought forth charges of Mexican depravity and violence, a theme which became pervasive once Anglos made closer contact with the state's Hispanic population following the war. In the crisis of the moment, firebrands spoke alarmingly of savage, degenerate, half-civilized, and barbarous Mexicans committing massacres and atrocities at Goliad and the Alamo.[43] Even worse, whites conjured up ideas of slave uprisings and possible alliances between slave rebels and Mexicans whom whites considered to be infused with African blood anyway. Entrepreneur James Morgan reported that slaves high upon the Trinity were daringly seeking to enlist the Coshatti [Coushatta] Indians and come down and murder the inhabitants in the Galveston region and join the Mexicans.[44] A resolution adopted by citizens meeting in Brazoria in March 1836 warned in consternation: "We have moreover been appraised of the horrid purpose of our treacherous and bloody enemy, to unite in his ranks, and as instruments of his unholy and savage work, the Negroes, whether slave or free, thus lighting the torch of war, in the bosoms of our domestic circles."[45]

Such talk may have been part of the hysteria that ordinarily accompanies war propaganda anywhere. But in any case, some whites were already regarding Mexicans as cruel enough to be considered less than human, and thus dispensable, like Indians, Africans, and animals. Reminiscing about his role in the struggle between Texas and Mexico, Creed Taylor recalled: "I thought I could shoot Mexicans as well as I could shoot Indians, or deer, or turkey; and so I rode away to a war."[46] Similarly, eighty-year-old Sion R. Bostick of San Saba County reminisced in 1900 that, although he did not know the real causes of the conflict, he joined it as "I thought I could kill Mexicans as easily as I could deer and turkeys."[47]

What whites found in the Texas experience during these first fifteen years was that Mexicans were primitive beings who during a century of residence in Texas had failed to improve their status and environment. Mexicans were religious pagans, purposelessly indolent and carefree, sexually remiss, degenerate, depraved, and questionably human. The haunting prospect of being ruled by such people indefinitely explains in part the Texian movement for independence in 1836.

Historians, however, have not paid due attention to these attitudes as factors in the movement for independence, for to do so is to come close to labeling the first generation of Texans as racists. White racism toward the indigenous Mexican population, some would maintain, did not develop until after an extended period of interaction between Texans and Mexicans. Not until decades later, others contend, did science postulate the biological inferiority of certain peoples, thereby begetting racist practices. Yet such arguments have ignored the baneful ubiquity of race in the forging of the American national character, have neglected the psychological implications of its presence, and are unattentive to the deep-seated resentment whites felt toward darker-skinned people whenever they came in contact with them. They have overlooked the motivating force of white supremacy and the compelling need of white America to press ahead with the task of "civilizing" colored peoples and what they stood for.

Dismissing racial prejudice means not taking account of Americans' psychic character as they came to interact with Mexicans in Texas. Admittedly, racism was not *the* cause of the Texas Revolution, but very certainly, it was *very* prominent as a promoting and underlying cause. Its roots were planted in the unique psychohistorical experience of the white Texas pioneers and settlers.

And indeed, in the heat of the crisis, leaders of the revolution revealed feelings about race that surely contributed to their strike for independence. Stephen F. Austin, despite his capacity to understand a culture "different" from his and assimilate into that culture with versatility, nevertheless revealed latent racist feelings as the combat raged. It was, he said, one of barbarism waged by a "mongrel Spanish-Indian and negro race, against civilization and the Anglo American race."[48] David G. Burnet, president of the *ad interim* revolutionary government, wrote to Senator Henry Clay: "The causes which have led to this momentous act are too numerous to be detailed in a single letter; but one general fact may account for all; the utter dissimilarity of character between the two people, the Texians and the Mexicans. The first are principally Anglo Americans; the others a mongrel race of degenerate Spaniards and Indians more depraved than they."[49] Much later, it was admitted that among the main reasons for the origins of the conflict was the "insuperable aversion" to social amalgamation between whites and Mexicans: "the colonists from the North were somewhat homogeneous in blood and color; the Mexicans, a mongrel breed of negroes, Indians and Spaniards of the baser sort."[50]

Thus, beneath the talk of oppression lingered the underpinnings of white supremacy and racial antipathy. In truth, the Texans never experienced oppression like that of others who have risen in rebellion. The Mexican government was thousands of miles away, afflicted with internal problems, and unable to pay proper attention to what was transpiring in Texas. Culturally, the Americans got along well with the *criollo* elite. In fact, after the revolution, the *criollos*, who closely resembled Anglos in racial makeup, were comfortably fitted into white society. Moreover, wherever Anglos went individually, and found themselves in a minority, they adjusted adequately to Mexican culture (despite harboring racist feelings). This was the case in the next decades in El Paso, Santa Fe, and Los Angeles.

But in Coahuila y Tejas, Anglos were dealing primarily not with *criollos*, but with mixed-blood (or "mongrel") Mexicans. And, by 1836, Texas was very different from later Southwestern settings. Though Texas was not legally American, it might as well have been. It was "white" spiritually, attitudinally, politically, socially, economically, and demographically—an American entity all to itself. These circumstances, in which Texians of diverse social standing thought of themselves as "white people" instead of individuals, incited the daring and massive quest for supremacy over barren wastes and Mexicanos.

Which is to say that the Texas Revolution was one of racial adjustment. For Anglo-Texans to have accepted anything other than "white supremacy and civilization" was to submit to Mexican domination and to admit that Americans were willing to become like Mexicans. The prospect of being dominated by such untamed, uncivil, and disorderly creatures made a contest for racial hegemony almost inevitable.

2. Niggers, Redskins, and Greasers: Tejano Mixed-Bloods in a White Racial State

Independence signaled an open invitation for other Anglos to come to Texas. Thousands responded, filling in the spaces of the Republic's eastern regions, then penetrating the Béxar, Goliad, and Victoria areas where the majority of Mexicanos resided. There, in the 1840s and 1850s, the greatest contact between the two peoples occurred and therefore the opportunity presented itself for comparison of civilization. From the San Antonio area, Anglos drifted gradually toward South Texas and entered that region of the state in force after the Mexican War of 1846–1848. West Texas remained a faraway land, but many passed through it in some government capacity or as itinerants heading for California in the late 1840s and 1850s. Hence, in the period between 1836 and 1860, white settlers and travelers were having the first significant face-to-face contact with Mexicans. It was during this time that they elaborated most precisely the distinctions between Mexicans and themselves.

For the most part, they continued to see Tejanos in images similar to those that others had conjured up between 1821 and 1836. This was natural, for the majority of those who came to Texas between the Revolution and the Civil War originated in the Upper South and the slave plantation systems of states fronting the Atlantic and Gulf coasts. A large number were from Alabama and Tennessee; others were pioneer Kentuckians or Missourians, while Georgia and Mississippi contributed a substantial share.[1] These sectionally oriented people, like those before them, brought with them their time-honored conventions related to race and culture, through which they evaluated Hispanic society. Consequently, the unflattering image formed before the revolution persisted essentially unchanged following firsthand association.

The physical features of Mexicans which had provoked wry comments from prerevolutionary settlers were the continued subject of the post-independence generation's observations. Actually, the physical affinity with the darker races of America was only one aspect of the total image Anglos held of Tejanos, and comments about it were invariably accompanied by discussions of Mexican cultural traits (about which Anglos spoke extensively). Nonetheless, that difference from themselves was a prominent one, enough that it brought out the most sensitive inner feelings Anglos held toward race.

Uppermost among the things related to race that took up space in the writings of antebellum observers were the ancestry, bodily forms, and complexion of Tejanos. Among the Mexicans of the Republic, noted one newspaper in 1837, such racial variety prevailed that it was difficult to distinguish the Spaniard from the "wild man."[2] Prince Carl of Solms-Braunfels, a popular authority on life in Texas, concurred. Mexicanos came in all mixtures of blood, he pointed out, "from the European-looking hidalgo, who can trace his ancestors to a real family, to the uncivilized, wild shepherd, whose color can hardly be distinguished from that of the Indian."[3] In their multiracial nature, the Mexicans were a different sort of people and did not approximate the Americans' ideal of racial excellence.

What Texans further perceived in this mixture were salient traces of the "redskin" and the "nigger." The kinship between Tejanos and Indians, especially, stimulated extensive commentary among both itinerants and settlers. Features, countenance, and the straight, coarse, black hair, for example, revealed to them the Indian inheritance.[4] "They are of mongrel blood the Aztec predominating," asserted Gilbert D. Kingsbury, writing about the Mexicans of Brownsville in the early 1860s. "These degraded creatures are mere pilferers, scavengers and vagabonds downright barbarians but a single remove above the Digger Indians, hanging like vermin on the skirts of civilization—a complete pest to humanity."[5]

Because Mexicans were preponderantly *mestizos*, they did not display conspicuous negroid physical features. Characteristics traceable to their negroid ancestry had probably been diluted by the nineteenth century; the years of repeated intermixture among *castas* had produced Mexicans more Indian than Spanish or African. Nevertheless, the black component could be detected, and allusions to the "half-negro, half-Indian greaser" and Mexicans of "mixed Indian and African blood" were not absent from the literature of the era.[6] Whites never grappled with questions about the origins of the Mexicans' physical properties. Unequivocally, Mexicans descended from Indians, with Africans making an addition.

A related topic of much interest and elucidation was color. What whites were especially sensitive to in connection with interracial sex was that the offspring were not whites but colored people. Certainly, Tejanos did not look like Anglos, and the physical connection to Indian and black left no doubt as to whom Mexicans more closely resembled. Most observers, whether travelers or natives, noted the obvious, considering Tejanos as having bronze complexions, as being of a copper color, of being of tawny hue, or simply as having the color of Native Americans.[7] The more opinionated among them described Tejanos as being "fully as dark as Indians."[8]

Beyond this, fixed perceptions about Indians were transposed and cross-culturally referred. The same "olive" color whites observed in the Indians of the seaboard states, for example, they attributed to the Mexicans of Texas. Frederick Law Olmsted, reporting meticulously on the Mexicans of Central Texas during his trip to the state in the mid-fifties, met an elderly Mexican woman "strikingly Indian in feature, her hair, snow white, flowing thick over the shoulders, contrasting strongly with the olive skin." The complexion of the young *señoritas* he likewise thought "clear, and sometimes fair, usually a blushing olive."[9]

The contemptuous word *greaser* which whites used to identify Mexicans may well have applied to Indians as well, since the Indians' olive color was thought to be a result of their practice of anointing their skins with oils and greases.[10] John C. Reid, passing through Texas as a prospective settler in the 1850s, sought to ascertain the origin of the application of the word upon finding that male Mexicans from Texas to the Pacific coast were called "greasers" and the females "greaser women." He failed to find a satisfactory explanation, learning only that it had something to do with the similarity between the Mexicans' color and that of grease. Another transient, commenting upon the vocabulary used in the El Paso region, supported this explanation: "A 'greaser' was a Mexican—originating in the filthy, greasy appearance of the natives."[11]

Then, there were those others who perceived a vestige of the Africans' coloring in Mexican *castas* as well. One traveler noted, for example, that the range of Mexicans' hues extended to African jet.[12] Justice of the Peace Adolphus Sterne, celebrating in 1842 the rites of matrimony between a Tejano, apparently a *criollo* of the upper class, and a white woman, noticed others of the groom's compatriots in the assemblage who were apparently *mestizos*. "If their hair would be a little curly," he remarked, "they would be taken anywhere for Negroes."[13] Similarly, Benjamin F. McIntyre, a Union officer in Civil

War Brownsville, conjectured that "Africa might lay some little claim" to the Mexicans' color.[14] Actually, not too many others made such an association, at least not so explicitly. In the last analysis, however, the Tejanos' pigmentation served to stimulate similar attitudes, even if a physical resemblance between Tejano and Negro was remote. As Oscar M. Addison put it in a letter to his brother, the Brownsville Mexicans in the 1850s were of "a class, inferior to common nigers [*sic*]."[15]

Then again, the unhygienic nature that white consciousness associated with the skin color of blacks was very naturally extended to Mexicanos. To whites, dark colors connoted filth and therefore Mexicans were a dirty, putrid people, existing in squalor. Thus observers made statements about Mexicans having habits "as filthy as their persons" or living in the "most shocking state of filth."[16] When a cholera epidemic plagued San Antonio in 1849, it hit the Mexican population especially hard. "If you could see the manner in which they live," one visitor commented, "you wouldn't for a moment wonder at their having the colera."[17]

Manifestly, spin-offs from racial attitudes developed and cultivated through repeated interaction with colored peoples on the western frontier were being bestowed upon another caste in a different setting. As Olmsted reported in his notes on Texas society of the 1850s, Mexicans were regarded as "degenerate and degraded Spaniards" or, perhaps, "improved and Christianized Indians." Generally, their tastes and social instincts were like those of Africans. "There are thousands in respectable social positions [in Mexico] whose color and physiognomy would subject them, in Texas, to be sold by the sheriff as negro-estrays who cannot be allowed at large without detriment to the commonwealth," he concluded.[18]

In view of the Southern presumption that individuals with any noticeable trace of African blood were blacks and given the contempt whites had for Indian "half-breeds," it is not surprising that "niggers," "redskins," and "greasers" intimately intermingled in the Anglo-Texan mind. Moreover, whites considered racial mixing a violation of austere moralistic codes. According to Joseph Eve, U.S. chargé d'affaires to the Republic, the Texans regarded Mexicans as a race of "mongrels" composed of Spanish, Indian, and African blood.[19] To Francis S. Latham, traveling in Texas in 1842, Mexicanos were nothing else than "the mongrel and illicit descendants of an Indian, Mexican and Spanish, pencilled with a growing feintline of the Anglo Saxon ancestry."[20] Such feelings about "mongrels" stemmed from the extensive lore American culture had developed concerning the undesirability and supposed peril of miscegenation, especially between whites and blacks. Certainly, the mixed-blood nature of Tejanos concerned Anglo-Americans because of their cultural aversion to interracial passion, a subject upon which whites expressed themselves adeptly, albeit with no scientific basis. According to white beliefs, Mexicans resembled the degenerates from whom they descended. Although they inherited both the faults and the good qualities of their ancestors, unfortunately, the darker traits predominated, so that Mexicans by nature were superstitious, cowardly, treacherous, idle, avaricious, and inveterate gamblers.[21] Miscegenation was a very serious matter which held great implications for civilization. William H. Emory, surveying the boundary between the United States and Mexico, related this idea in an incidental remark included as part of his report, finished during the Franklin Pierce administration. Attributing the decline and fall of Spanish domination in Texas and the borderlands to a "baneful" cohabitation between whites and Indians, he continued:

Where practical amalgamation of races of different color is carried [out] to any extent, it is from the absence of the women of the cleaner race. The white makes his alliance with his darker partner for no other purpose than to satisfy a law of nature, or to acquire property, and when that is accomplished all affection ceases. Faithless to his vows, he passes from object to object with no other impulse than the gratification arising from novelty, ending at last in emasculation and disease, leaving no progeny at all; or if any, a very inferior and syphilitic race. Such are the favors extended to the white man by the lower and darker colored races, that this must always be the course of events, and the process of absorption can never work any beneficial change. One of the inevitable results of intermarriage between races of different color is infidelity. The offspring have a constant tendency to go back to one or the other of the original stock; that in a large family of children, where the parents are of a mixed race but yet of the same color, the children will be of every color, from dusky cinnamon to chalky white. This phenomenon, so easily explained without involving the fidelity of either party, nevertheless produces suspicion followed by unhappiness, and ending in open adultery.[22]

This sort of pseudoscience dictated the status of mixed-blood Tejanos in a white state.

In the period that followed the Revolution until about the time of the Civil War, then, whites had made unprecedented contact with Mexicans, primarily in Central and South Texas. Attitudes toward blacks, Indians, color, and miscegenation—with their genesis in the racial interaction that was part of the frontier Americanization process before 1821—provided a basis for regarding Mexicans as kin to "redskins" and "niggers."[23]

After the transitory decades of the 1860s and 1870s, Texas entered the initial phases of commercial farming, industrialization, and urbanization, and the railroad brought different sections into closer contact. These developments attracted more people into cosmopolitan San Antonio, where they came in contact with the Hispanic *barrio*; sent farmers and ranchers into West Texas, where they encountered the established Mexicans of the El Paso Valley and newer immigrants from Mexico searching for work; and, most significantly, pushed fortune seekers into the major pocket of Mexican concentration in South Texas. In this period, it was newcomers and travelers who carefully detailed the connection among Afro-Americans, Indians, and Mexicanos and the ramifications of racial mixing. Natives no longer concerned themselves with the question of mongrelization. The way they felt about it was so institutionalized as to be conventional. It was understood that Mexicans were not of the same racial stock as white Americans; there was no need to discuss the matter.

But if whites did not overstate their feelings, they remained ever cognizant of the Mexicans' conglomerate nature. They continued to be aware of the Indian component, some referring to Mexicans as the descendants of Montezuma and labeling them "Aztecs."[24] Inherited traits told others of a darker blood, or as a writer of San Antonio argued in 1877, of a gentler Indian with no claim to the name of "Mexican."[25] Keener observers like Nathaniel A. Taylor, a newspaperman with an itch for traveling, could be quite graphic, as he was in describing Bexareños in the late seventies: "Their hair is coarse, coal-black and straight as an Indian's. Their cheek-bones and noses are generally prominent, and many of the latter are aquiline. They seem to me to take much more after the Indian than the Spaniard. I have indeed seen scores of them who were as much like the Digger as possible."[26] The Anglos of San Angelo identified the Mexican residents in 1889 with the native Indians of subtropical Mexico. They were, according to J. E. MacGowan, a visiting reporter from Tennessee, "a race of mongrels, chiefly Aztecs, with a sprinkle of Spanish and Negro."[27]

Very little appeared in the last three decades of the century con-
necting Mexicans with Africans, however. Neither outsiders nor na-
tive Texans had much to say about this point. In fact, not even the color of the Mexican provoked the earlier
commentary. Taylor, who had insisted on the physical similarity of
Bexareños and Indians, explained tersely that the color of Tejanos
stretched from that of new-tanned leather to a peculiar reddish
black.[28] The observers expressing the stronger responses tended to
be outsiders who discerned shades already familiar to long-time
Texans. Thus MacGowan, the Chattanooga journalist in San Angelo
in 1889, reported that the local Tejanos were "dark to the point of
blackness."[29] An easterner in El Paso in 1893 informed an acquaintance back home that some of the *señoras* in the city were "as dark as
the darkest Indian you ever saw."[30]

But in no way did the lack of discussion imply that Texans had
lost their sensitivity to the significance of color, for they remained
acutely conscious of its meaning. Color still symbolized the essence
of what Texans and other Americans regarded as good and evil—a
psychological connection traceable to Elizabethan England. As the
Southern Intelligencer noted in 1865, "white was the emblem of
light, religious purity, innocence, faith, joy and life," indicating
integrity in the judge, humanity in the sick, and chastity in the
woman. Black was its opposite, it "expressed the earth, darkness,
mourning, wickedness, negation, death, and was appropriate to the
Prince of Darkness."[31] Color was a demarcation between the desirable and the undesirable, the acceptable and the unacceptable, the
tolerable and the intolerable. It could also be a blotch distinguishing
between white and colored peoples.

Thus, even if the Texans were reticent in commenting on the
Mexicans' color, their penchant was to associate white and dark
skin with superiority and decadence, respectively. Color distinguished characteristics, traits, and attributes among races, according
to the *San Antonio Herald* of 1868. The paper argued that blond,
fair-skinned, blue-eyed races were given to doubt, to discussion and
investigation, to invention and improvement, were aggressive in
their tendencies; hence their rapid advancement. Dark-skinned,
black-eyed, black-haired races, on the other hand, were conservative in their tendencies, seldom deviated from old established principles, customs, and religions; hence their lesser progress.[32] In this
thinking, swarthy Mexicans obviously fell squarely in the degenerate category attached to the darker shades of color. Backwardness
was equated with Mexicanness.

By the same impulse, Anglos continued to relate skin pigmentation to dirt, and Mexicans therefore were associated with filth. The *Brownsville Ranchero* complained that the local population of blacks and Mexicans in 1867 lived among a large colony of dogs that proved a "thoroughly intolerable" nuisance to the town's white citizenry.[33] Mexicans in Texas were so commonly regarded as unhygienic that in one case in 1871, they were held up as the epitome of slovenliness. In a certain East Texas area, editorialized the *San Antonio Express*, "the hogs lived as much in the houses . . . and from the similarity it was hard to tell where the hogs left off and inhabitants began." Those denizens, concluded the paper, were "not one whit above the lower class of Mexicans."[34]

The newspapers were elaborating on something which most Texans regarded as inherent to the Mexican character. Outsiders encountering Mexicanos for the first time were even more emphatic in depicting them as extremely filthy. Among these was a military officer, who, in 1891, reported the Mexicans near LaGrulla in South Texas as having a total disregard for all the basics of hygiene. "We saw children whose scabby heads hadn't been washed for six weeks, and others, suffering from catarrh, whose faces could be cleaned by nothing but a stream of water from a fire engine," he said. The adults were no better off, he continued, though they lived amid the bloom of roses, morning glories, honeysuckles, balsams, and oleanders.[35]

Thus, color was a basic determinant of the way Anglos saw Mexicans. Anglos were not going to regard as equals people whom they thought to be colored, whom they therefore considered uncivilized, and whom they connected with filth and its foul implications. What Olmsted had said about the Texans' regard for Tejanos at mid-century was still reported about Anglo-Tejano relations in the latter decades of the century: that Mexicans were held in no higher esteem than blacks and Indians, that Mexican disfranchisement was attempted because Mexicans were of Indian ancestry, and that Jim Crow signs read "for Mexicans" instead of "for Negroes" in South Texas.[36] Though the idea was no longer vocalized as often as before the Civil War, it was understood that only minor differences separated "greasers" from "redskins" and "niggers."

The same thing happened with the provocative question of miscegenation. Whites no longer focused on the bane of Indian, African, and Mexican mixing as much as before, nor on the bad qualities inherited.[37] Nor did they pen passionate outbursts comparable to those of Emory in the 1850s. But as in the case of color, the absence of hard discussion did not signify a new tolerance. Thus when Mary S.

Helm took up the subject in 1878 while writing an essay on early Texas history, she argued that the instinct of races never died out. Endowed with incredible and inexhaustible energy, Anglo-Americans never turned back despite the severity of obstacles, she was convinced. The modern Mexicans, in contrast, were the debris of several inferior and degraded races, including a mix of African, Indian, Spanish, and Moorish. "Both physically and mentally," Helm maintained, "they are the very antithesis of the Anglo American."[38]

The *San Antonio Express* of December 15, 1890, seemed to agree. It editorialized that only in one case did miscegenation between whites and Indians produce creditable results. That was in the case where whites intermarried with the descendants of Pocahontas. In that one case, the mixed-blood offspring could claim a right to democratic aristocracy, but in no other instance, the paper lectured, had it been possible to graft a superior on an inferior race and produce descendants who partook more largely of the physical and mental peculiarities of the superior than of the inferior race.[39]

Following the Texas Revolution, then, white settlers continued to perceive the Mexicans' color, their mixed blood, and their supposed lack of civilization in ways that confirmed old notions about race. Their own children adopted more or less the same attitudes, and such views were buttressed by racial interaction with Mexicans on a color frontier. Prospective immigrants in the post–Civil War period were exposed to discourses in popular journals on the terrible results of miscegenation in Latin America. The *Southern Review,* for example, published an editorial condemning "mongrelism," expressing the attitudes of whites in general toward the Latin race in America:

> An admixture of two unequal races is therefore a cancer, an unpardonable sin against mankind and against nature, which has launched an ever flaming curse on all such connections; inasmuch as she lets the mongrels invariably inherit all the vices and evil traits of both races and rarely, or never, any of the good. Nature absolutely disallows the adulteration of blood; and herein she shows herself to be an aristocrat of the purest water. Every violation of these laws she visits in the most condign and pitiless manner.[40]

Other national journals, including *Harper's Weekly* and the *Overland Monthly,* as well as publications within Texas[41] served as formulators of opinion or reflected it. Most of their discourses conformed to the standard white image of Mexicans as a folk resulting from villainous miscegenation. It was within this framework that Mexican Americans in Texas were considered throughout the century. True, Anglos also seized upon other dimensions of the Mexican nature to support their comments on Mexican inferiority—on their oppression by church and state in Mexico, on cultural traits, on an alleged violent disposition, and so on—but physical peculiarities, such as the Mexicans' "colored" pigmentation, were constant reminders of the link between darkness and filth, death, and other evil things. Whites did not purposely invent sordid stereotypes; their comments on the Mexican image, often venomous ones, reflected a real state of racial thinking. In the nineteenth century, white society did have the freedom to be prejudiced without fear of legal sanctions, and the actions of whites toward those they despised often corresponded closely to their attitudes. Their racial and nationalist distaste for Mexicans, thus, was a major cause of the degradation of Tejanos during the entire century.

3. An Indolent People

Implicit in the Anglo concept of race were certain ingrained cultural values fundamentally a part of the American ethos. The ethnocentric whites necessarily saw Tejano culture as different—distinct from American customs, principles, and traditions. Throughout the century, whites spoke of Mexican docility, ignorance, decadence, mediocrity, antagonism toward work, submission to vice, and hedonistic proclivities. Mexicans seemed a culturally wanton people.

Hence, biological difference was only one aspect of the total image whites had of Mexicans, for culture also made up a large segment of that picture. In the comparison Anglos made, the cultural structure of Mexicans was the antithesis of theirs. Where whites were energetic, Mexicans seemed backward; where whites were ambitious and aggressive, Mexicans seemed apathetic and complacent; where whites considered themselves inventive, Mexicans seemed anachronistic; and where whites knew their direction, Mexicans appeared to be going nowhere. When juxtaposed with Mexicano society (as, indeed, when compared with the black and red societies that incidentally inhabited the state also), white culture appeared much more advanced, more progressive, and more civilized.

In the period between 1836 and the Civil War, Mexicans came under the close scrutiny of ethnocentric whites (usually travelers) in all sections of the state, and especially in Central Texas, where the two cultures had the greatest amount of contact in the 1840s and 1850s. But everywhere, Anglos saw Mexicans as mirror opposites of themselves. Unlike Anglos, who saw work as the avenue to wealth and improvement, Mexicans seemed possessed of an aversion to toil. They subscribed to indolence and indifference and all the vices associated therewith. In the Rio Grande Valley, the very shadow of work overpowered Tejano ranchers, reported one scrutinizer, their sole arduous undertaking being leisure.[1] Olmsted described the

Mexicans of Nacogdoches "leaning against posts and looking on in grand decay," while those in San Antonio had adopted "a free-and-easy, loloppy sort of life." He found them engrossed in "jollity" and "sleepy comfort," and "the whole picture lacked nothing that is Mexican."² The Mexicans of El Paso were no different. One of their more notable characteristics was indolence, reported a traveler in 1849.³ In all sections, Mexicans seemed to lack the spirit of enterprise, the drive, the zeal common to American civilization. Instead, they were shiftless and unambitious and wallowed in the direst poverty, making no efforts to improve their dismal status, to educate themselves, to excel in the arts of accomplishment in civilized life, or to "procure the comforts of life."⁴ They just went along living in the present, unworried about *mañana*.

Owing to their passivity and complacency, their adherence to traditionalism, and their reluctance to earn a living in meaningful ways, Mexicans eked out a scanty day-to-day existence, which, according to Anglo descriptions, was all they desired out of life. An anonymous traveler in 1837 opined that Bexareños did not trouble themselves about the future so long as they were satisfied with a bare living for the present. They required only small quantities of corn, and since their animal food was easily gained, they did not exert themselves beyond necessity.⁵ They made it on the "smawlest quanty [sic] of food possible to sustain life,"⁶ wrote a visitor to San Antonio in 1855. Undeniably, concurred McIntyre, the Union soldier in Civil War Brownsville, the subsistence needs of local Mexicans were most simple. "A little bread and beef which is purchased each morning at market answers for their daily food."⁷

Furthermore, whites construed the *jacales* Tejanos inhabited as a further manifestation of the backwardness and noninventiveness of Mexican culture. In their opinion, Mexicans lacked the instinctual resolution to build the most essential dwellings to deter the elements. Because Mexicans were too idle to erect more comfortable cabins, asserted A. B. Lawrence, a Texas visitor in 1840, they chose rather to endure inclement weather.⁸ They lived in wretched hovels, in deplorable cabins, and in forlorn-looking huts. "These homes are composed of rustic straw works or mud bricks called *adobes*," wrote Brownsville resident Teresa Vielé. "There in one apartment are frequently found five generations living together eking out an indolent existence on a mild diet of ground corn, eggs, and milk."⁹

The carts that Mexican freighters used to transport supplies from the interior to the coast were seen as further evidence of the character and habits of Mexicans. The looks and construction of the carts revealed the technological primitivism of a misplaced culture, for even at mid-century, the vehicles smacked of obsolescence. Americans were too much committed to advancement, too much imbued with the spirit of progress to engage in any business redolent of the past, declared John Russell Bartlett, a traveler in the state in the 1850s. "The idea of carrying on commerce with oxcarts, making 130 miles in six days over an excellent road might do for the past century, not for the steam and lightning age."[10]

Instead of applying themselves to the task of self-improvement, Mexicans had an inclination for wringing enjoyment from misery. As whites saw it, Mexicans were too much given to lower pleasures, approaching life with carefree abandon. Music, hunting, love, and cards comprised much of their existence.[11] In particular, Tejanos had a craving for gambling, which, according to numerous commentators, was a marked trait of their nationality.[12] "A passion for gambling is found almost nowhere except among the Mexicans," noted Victor Bracht, a recent immigrant to the Republic of Texas. "They are addicted to it in a higher degree."[13]

When it came to priorities, elaborated William A. McClintock, an army man passing through San Antonio on his way to participate in the Mexican War, there was no doubt that Mexicans preferred the local gambling establishment to the church: "I yesterday saw (and the like may be seen on any Sabbath), many Mexicans leave chapel even before mass was concluded and repair to the gaming table; where they spent the remainder of the day perhaps the whole night." Labor to them was a last resort, he exclaimed.[14] In El Paso, too, Mexicans displayed a similar penchant. Albert D. Richardson arrived there in 1859 and found gambling universal, from the boys' game of pitching *cuartillas* (three-cent coins) to the great saloons where huge piles of silver were staked at monte.[15] What remained unexplained by McClintock and Richardson, as well as many other whites in the nineteenth century, was how such indolent people were able to amass so much money to stake at the gambling table.

As before the revolution, then, whites continued to see Mexicans as culturally decadent, a perception that jibed with their view that Mexicans were racially inferior. By defining themselves as a people on the move, and imputing to Mexicans degenerate values, they reaffirmed the domination of civilization over nature. Anglos also rationalized displacing Tejanos. It was, after all, in the 1840s and 1850s that Americans were drenched with the spirit of Manifest Destiny and were even thinking beyond those areas populated by

Mexicans in Texas. If Mexicans could not keep pace with Yankee progress, or improve their standard of living, it was their own fault, not that of white America.

In the latter decades of the century, while whites paid less attention to Mexican mixed-blood degeneracy, they took more notice of alleged Tejano cultural decadence. The Mexicans' cultural ways attracted the notice of both the native population and travelers; the former because Texans were in closer contact than before with Mexicans, especially in the border areas where Tejanos were most visibly concentrated, and the latter because Mexicans represented something novel about the unsettled West. It was indeed the time when the reading public outside the state was avidly consuming the picturesqueness of the West.

For the outsider, San Antonio presented the ideal setting for contrasts of civilizations. Located conveniently in the central part of the state and featuring a mix of ethnic groups, it invited inspection. Every conceivable contrast which Anglos wished to see between Mexican and Anglo cultures could be discerned. Inertness was compared with vigor, stagnation with progress, the anachronistic with the future. The old and new coexisted, as the names, manners, features, costumes, and language of the days of Cortez and Pizarro blended with contemporary styles and idioms.[16] Primitivism also jostled with modernity. In Laredito, the Mexican section of San Antonio, the life of the eighteenth century still prevailed without taint of modernism, observed Edward King and J. Wells Champney in 1874. The Mexican could not be made to see that "his slow, primitive ways, his filth and lack of comfort, are not better than the frugal decency and careful home management of the Germans and Americans who surround him."[17]

The alien and the familiar contrasted sharply in San Antonio. On Saturday, when the marketplace opened for business, observers were reminded of the customs of the old Spanish town, said James L. Rock and W. I. Smith in *Southern and Western Texas Guide for 1878*. Meandering through the streets were beggars on foot and on horseback, swarthy Mexicans and dark-eyed *señoritas* with peppery vegetables, and peddlers selling dime packs of hay, stove-length faggots, and bundled stacks of green maize, while *señoras* on the plaza in front of the cathedral walls served black coffee and chocolate.[18] "These greasers are not inclined to assimilate their customs and modes to those of whites," but persisted in their old ways, asserted a *Harper's New Monthly Magazine* correspondent in 1879.[19]

The town offered abundant material for comparisons between

Mexican and American cultures. As E. V. Smally wrote in the *New York Tribune*:

> It is a city of the most striking contrasts. Here our pushing Western civilization comes in contact with the sleepy, dead alive, half-civilization of Mexico. The Palace car meets the ox team and the panniered donkey; the New York drummer, arrayed in faultless garments from the Broadway shops, jostles in narrow streets the *ranchero* in *poncho* and *sombrero*; and the Boston tourist, running away from consumption, encounters the blanketed Indian of the plains. Here are fine stone mansions that would not be out of place in the loveliest suburbs of Philadelphia, and here are Mexican huts thatched with cornstalks, beside which the dwellings Stanley saw in Uganda were models of comfort. Fine modern churches, with carpeted aisles and cushioned pews, stand in sight of a venerable Spanish cathedral where swarthy penitents, muffled in shawls, crouch on the stone floor and tell their beads. Here are spacious stores, filled with as costly goods as can be found in Eastern cities, daily newspapers, banks, water works, gas works, telegraph offices, a club and a theatre; and there are quaint and dirty little Mexican shops, adobe buildings with loop-holed battlements, scarred with bullet marks, along[side] wagon trains from Chihuahua and Monterrey bringing silver and taking back cotton, soldiers, priests, nuns, negroes, greasers, half-breed Comanches, dirt, dogs and fleas.[20]

But itinerants did not restrict themselves to old historic Béxar, for they drew conclusions about Mexicans in West Texas which identified them also as the embodiment of a dysfunctional culture. In 1869, Mexican residents of San Elizario were accused of "too much indolence. They are priest-ridden, without schools or ambition and have little conception of Yankee progress."[21] In El Paso, Mexicans waited patiently and complacently for life to slip away after its own fashion, noted a correspondent for the *New York Commercial Advertiser* in 1887; they took no note of time but remained happy and unworried despite the obvious misfortunes afflicting them.[22] In 1890 in Eagle Pass, Mexicans were said to live in a primitive manner, presenting a mixture of poverty, ignorance, and dirt in comparison to the wealth, culture, and refinement of whites.[23] In these western regions as well, Mexicans led a life that contrasted greatly with that of Texans.

It was the local population which in this era more prominently asserted the notion of the Tejanos' indolence and accompanying vices. This was especially the case in South Texas, where the major pocket of Tejano residence was situated, and in West Texas, where Mexicans had lived apart from the centers of white society. For it was into those regions that Anglos were moving during the 1870s and 1880s. Thus, much of the rhetoric about defective cultural values corresponded to the need to overcome Mexican American cultural pre-eminence. As things stood at this time in many parts of those sections, it was a world turned upside down, where more Mexicans than Anglos lived. Here were new frontiers from which whites heard calls for redemption. Hence, all the emphasis on the cultural wantonness of Mexicans. It was necessary to justify the subjugation of the external world—the chaparral, the mesquite, the Mexicans—else chaos would continue instead of civilized order. Simultaneously, there remained the necessity for a pool of menials with meager needs—who could be paid little since their bodily requirements were elemental.

Native Texans thus put a great amount of stress on Mexican indifference toward material improvement. Like their antebellum predecessors, postbellum commentators maintained that time other than the present did not worry Mexicans. "They live a dolce far niente life caring naught for the morrow, but with cigarette in their mouth, calmly face the stern reality of today with that stoicism that they derive from their Indian ancestors," one writer proclaimed.[24] In the El Paso district, the masses in 1873 were reputedly a happy people; they concerned themselves only with today and considered any who contemplated the future crazy beyond all reach of hellebore (a drug for treating insanity).[25] The editors of the *El Paso Times* agreed in a story covering the relocation of Mexicans in old Fort Bliss following the destruction of homes in the *barrio* by a flood from the Rio Grande in 1897:

> The Mexican is by nature light hearted and the uneducated class live on the principle that "sufficient unto the day is the evil thereof." Fill their stomachs and give them plenty of sunshine today and they will not worry themselves about tomorrow's dinner. If you think the refugees at old Fort Bliss are mourning for their lost homes, go out there tonight and listen to the merry laughter, the music of the flute, violin, guitar and mandolin and watch the merry couples in the dance. Here and there you may find a thrifty old man and woman trying to

frown down the thoughtless merriment, but care finds a very
weak foothold at old Fort Bliss.[26]

Tejanos were so much resigned to what the day brought them,
the anti-Mexican sentiment continued, that they seemed content to
live in grinding privation. They meekly accepted their state of des-
titution, made no gestures toward overcoming the perplexities that
befell them, and adjusted to life without giving thought to improv-
ing their primitive manner of supplying their necessities. Hans
Mickle, a traveling correspondent for the San Antonio Express, conjectured in 1879 that a family of eight or ten along the border could
maintain itself all year on a small five-acre field, a few goats, a couple of old broken-down horses, two or three cows, and perhaps some
donkeys and then be perfectly content to live and die in a mud
jacal.[27] San Angelo Mexicans reportedly could subsist on a couple of
meals a day, usually of a biscuit made of flour set up on any old bit of
tin and baked in the ashes under live coals.[28]

So regardless of time and place, those who evaluated Tejano life
orientation thought the Mexicans to be people whose acceptance of
things as they were, in effect, was testimonial to the lesser nutrients
they needed for survival. In a racial order where Anglos dominated
Mexicans, a rationalization could be made for dual wage systems, for
example, because it was known that Mexicans subsisted on less.

Mexican homes as representatives of an antiquated and unen-
terprising culture continued to incur their share of judgments. Texans still considered jacales symbolic of Tejano backwardness, irresponsibility, and noninventiveness. Unlike other intimate aspects of
Tejano society which were shielded from public view, the jacal
stood out conspicuously, exposed as a special item or artifact for
study. Instead of seeing it as a type of housing made from available
materials and one which answered the needs of poor people in an
effective way, Anglos disparaged it. The grass and straw roofs, the
mesquite walls, the clay or mud floors, the makeshift furniture, and
other aspects of the domicile came in for ridicule. Anglos pointed to
it as an object of primitivism and backwardness, not as a product of
the Mexican capacity for improvisation.[29]

The Mexican jacal was one more feature that Anglos pointed to
as an illustration of the Tejano requirement for less. As Lee C.
Harby, the Harper's New Monthly Magazine journalist, rationalized
his concern for Mexicans who dwelled in those shelters: they met
their needs, he was convinced, and Tejanos were as calmly content
as their more comfortable neighbors.[30]

The argument that Mexican culture was firmly against innovation and deeply rooted in the past also applied to the Mexicans' farming methods. In South and West Texas, particularly, where Tejanos in the last decades of the century retained some acreage, whites considered Mexican agricultural techniques as passé as other aspects of Mexican culture. They accused Tejanos of using unscientific plans, imperfect systems of cultivation, and crude implements. Mexicans were some three hundred years behind the times, it was maintained, working their land as they had in the days of Cortez, relying on a plow composed simply of a crooked stick with an iron point. Consequently, much land still remained undeveloped, the Mexicans' backwardness having a retarding influence upon Anglo-Saxon progress.[31] Tejanos refused to profit from the newer technology of Anglo-Americans, whites insisted. "As long as they persist in following in the footsteps of their illustrious predecessors and use the crooked stick with a gato on the point of it for a plow, and continue to scratch over the surface of the ground in place of plowing deeply," reasoned "Vigilante," a correspondent for the *San Antonio Express*, "just that long will they expect to raise poor crops."[32]

Anglo insistence on the image of Mexicans as backward and primitive obviously provided some justification for relegating them to less desirable occupational functions. For if Tejanos did not have the intellectual capacity of whites, then they ought not to be employed in tasks requiring the complex calculations Anglos associated with themselves. From this it followed that some jobs were appropriately Mexican. In the Corpus Christi area, Mexicans were a necessary element where no other servants were available, argued Mary A. Sutherland, a long-time resident. Despite the Mexican's lack of reasoning power, she advised, he, "like the Chink," could learn his work, though there did exist a problem with irresponsibility. If instructed to start morning fires in midwinter, for example, he would continue until July unless stopped, she noted, or if ordered to irrigate the garden, he would continue doing so even in the midst of a downpour or even after the garden was inundated. Employers therefore had to keep a cautious vigil on the Mexicans, she advised.[33]

Considering the qualities of intellect and personality Texans attributed to Mexicans, it is not surprising to find Anglos writing discourses regarding the proper treatment of Mexican workers. Sheepraiser H. Bundy of the Pleasanton area took it upon himself to share with newcomers his familiarity with the Mexican sheepherder. Mexicans, Bundy advised whites entering the sheep business, were eminently acceptable as sheepherders. As a general rule, he declared, there was in Texas only one class of men that were natural-born shepherds. "If the designer of nature made the Mexican and had any one design in making him, he must have intended him to herd sheep." But because of certain idiosyncrasies in the Mexican character, admonished Bundy, the sheepraiser had to attend to the serious and difficult task of maintaining good relations with his shepherds. Since Mexicans spoke no English, the owner was compelled to speak Spanish, and there was no getting along with the workers peacefully unless one "talked their lingo." The ideal procedure, he instructed, was to learn the language through association (though books were acceptable as a second recourse), as in this way the Mexicans' nature and ways might also be learned. And how should they be managed? They were naturally suspicious and shy of Americans and were very superstitious, like other ignorant people. A few Mexicans could understand some English, and therefore there was need for caution, since imprudent remarks taken out of context could well offend or frighten the shepherd into quitting. Concerning the Mexicans' duties, a contract was imperative so that no misunderstandings would arise as to their commitments. As for their rations, there had to exist a definite understanding about what kind of food and how much they were to get per month. Here humanitarianism and empathy did not enter, for the Mexicans' austere and frugal diet dictated the owner's responsibility. They had few actual necessities of life, he related, and "they could live a week on what an American would eat in a day, and do well." And how should Mexicans be treated? "You will hear many say that you must treat them like dogs," Bundy warned, "but that depends upon how you treat your dogs. There is no human so low but who will appreciate kindness and wishes you to tell him of it if he does your work well." Punctuality in meeting appointments was essential, as was consistency in employer-employee relations. "Be as particular in little things with them as if they were of importance, for they are people of little things. Be firm, yet kind. No cursing; no swearing and charging around them," he ended.[34]

In taking such a paternalistic attitude toward Tejanos, Bundy and men of his ilk probably felt they were doing the proper and Christian thing. After all, they were coming to the assistance of culturally lost folks. Implicit in that compassion, however, was the belief that Mexicans were less deserving of humaneness and respect than members of white society.

At the same time that Anglos continued to understand Mexicans as culturally out of place, they held to the conviction that Tejanos, despite their poverty, spent their lives in frolic and gambling, *fiestas* and *fandangos*. Visiting whites had always attributed to Mexicans a unique predilection for gambling. Now, in the years after the Civil War, the local white population found them almost obsessed with the pastime. The notorious bandit Ben Thompson, for example, classified all Mexicanos as fervent gamblers. "No matter what the character, calling or profession, they all unite as monte players, and meet all on a perfect equality about the card-table," he claimed. Their inclination was to bet high when thinking they had the advantage, and they would risk their money, clothing, and anything else they had. In many instances, he related, he had known men to bet their liberty, and, losing, become peons.[35] In the same areas where whites said Tejanos were too lazy to work and were living in substandard conditions, they reported them to be all the more inclined to games of chance. In Laredo, noted a visitor in 1881, more money changed hands in a few hours at the Hancock, a saloon that had at least 120 faro tables, than in all the gambling halls of New Orleans and the cotton brokers as well.[36] Mexicans sallied forth at dusk, agreed a reporter for the *San Antonio Express*, to enjoy the many "gilded palaces" of the town and play cards, billiards, and pool until long after midnight. In the dance hall areas of some saloons, "women of the lowest order, and men after their kind" were the chief patrons.[37] In El Paso, whites similarly reported Mexicans engrossed in playing dice, faro, high-ball poker, draw-poker, and casino at the numerous gambling places. The familiar "immense pile of money" could be seen in many of these dens.[38]

So overpowering was the Mexicans' alleged obsession for the game that they could always come up with the money to visit the gaming table. Stressing the Mexicans' love for the cockfight, the humorists Alexander E. Sweet and John Armoy Knox elaborated that whatever the Mexicans' indigent circumstances, they could always draw upon their pawnbroker for the cost of a ticket to the cockpit on Sunday.[39] A Mexican might not be able to raise money for his dying grandmother, added the novelist Stephen Crane in 1899, upon visiting Béxar's Mexican quarter, where gambling houses appeared in abundance, but he could always stake himself for a game of monte.[40] In this distorted way Anglos explained the incongruency of an indigent people who nevertheless found means and ways to satiate a compulsion for revelry.

Besides being inveterate gamblers, Tejanos were also thought to hold perpetual *fiestas*. The *fiesta* was a national institution with Spanish-speaking people the world over, according to *San Antonio*

Express correspondent Mickle. Transmitted from Spain, the *fiesta* had continued in Texas under Spanish and Mexican rule, and now ostensibly flourished under American rule together with its accompanying *fandangos* and public gambling.[41] Those who touched on the celebrations of the various feast days failed to appreciate their cultural merits and instead identified them with the frivolous propensities of Tejanos. Another writer for the *San Antonio Express*, in describing the Fiesta de San Juan of 1876, expressed disbelief when seeing what transpired during the festivities: the old and feeble were temporarily transformed as they imbibed *aguardiente*; youths planted their *medios* (coins) on the gambling table to chance victory or defeat; *señoritas* dashed gaily by; gamblers attended to their stack of money; monte, keno, and lotteries attracted just about everyone; and children made confusion worse with their general merriment. The correspondent, signing himself "J," added his own impression: "It is a great period of fun—such fun as it is."[42]

"Don José," another *Express* reporter, found the Mexican population of San Diego in Duval County celebrating a similar *fiesta* in November 1880. It was all bustle and confusion, according to the correspondent, as "greasers" roamed about in delight, the plaza being dimly lit at night while a few monte banks lured unsuspecting patrons into gambling.[43]

Most often, when whites talked about Mexican lethargy and debauchery, they had in mind the regions of South and West Texas which they were penetrating in the waning decades of the century. It was those areas which now called out for order to replace disorder. As a reporter anticipated in 1881, it was only a matter of time until a radical change occurred in southwestern Texas, "when an English speaking and reading people will open up and develop the rich and hidden resources of this vast wilderness that is now infested by roaming Mexicans, rattlesnakes, and braying jackasses." White progress and ingenuity would supplant Mexican retrogression and anachronism, cities and towns would replace villages, and fenced farms would be cultivated where little brush-fenced patches stood. To see this change, he continued, the reader only had to visit Laredo, where the work had already commenced.[44] In 1889, the *Austin Statesman* announced that Laredo had in fact cast off the "indolent repose" of the Spanish-Indian civilization of a few years back and was now a thriving place.[45]

In El Paso, similarly, C. F. Drake, ex-president of the State Firemen's Association, who had been away for about fifteen years, returned in 1897 to find that whites had completely transformed the town for the better. Before the railroad, he noted, there existed only

> an adobe village, which differed in no particular from like settlements in Mexico, and which gave no evidence to the traveler that he had emerged from the land of the Montezumas and that he was beneath the protecting folds of Old Glory. An adobe *jacal* was the leading hostelry of the place, it was presided over by a lazy Mexican and his still less industrious wife. The business houses were but rough buildings, of which the better grade was given up entirely to saloons and gambling dens. The streets were deep in sand, and the people apparently deep in thought, but thoughts which perhaps never led them to conceive of any material change from their condition. Aside from the devout Catholic, who upon Sunday mornings and saints' day offered upon their voices in praise to their Creator, the large portion of the people spent the Sabbath in gaming and drinking. [Now, however, the city stands as a monument] to the energy and progressiveness of the American citizens, who, step by step, starting at the Atlantic ocean, overcoming every obstacle, and facing every danger, have paved the dense forests, mountain passes, and broad plains to the Pacific with a civilization that stands without an equal in history.[46]

Left unmentioned, of course, was the fact that Mexicans, in El Paso and in other regions of Texas, often composed the primary labor force responsible for those advances. Most Mexicanos got limited returns from that transformation, moreover, because Anglo concessions generally amounted to no more than that which they felt becoming to an indolent people with meager needs.

4. Defective Morality

Besides picturing Mexicans as culturally debased, Anglos also believed them to be morally defective. Historically, pioneers and settlers had seen other colored groups in the same way; thus the vision of the Mexican with defective morality conformed to previous patterns of race relations. Indians during the colonial period, for example, were used as a negative reference group to define white morality and sexuality (as well as other things). Part of the picture that emerged from the image Europeans formed of the "good" Indian and the "bad" Indian was that Native Americans practiced polygamy and engaged in sexual promiscuity. Colonists continued thereafter to depict the aborigines as the ones they had encountered in the initial contacts.[1] As for slaves, they were seen as licentious because whites refused to admit their own sexual aggressions,[2] and throughout the nineteenth century, Americans continued to attribute an amoral nature to black people. In those settings where Anglos encountered Mexicans, the latter also became objects for comparison as whites attempted to retain their own sense of virtue and morality. By projecting onto Mexicans what they did not wish to see in themselves, they sought reaffirmation of their righteousness. Mexicans were envisioned as morally corrupt, with a sense of propriety different from that of Anglos.[3]

Whites expressed their most revealing emotions about what they considered the moral perversity of Mexicanos during the decades before the Civil War. That was the time when white society was spreading throughout different regions of the state, making direct contact with Tejanos, and discerning the greatest differences between the two civilizations. Just as they found Mexicans biologically and culturally degenerate, so whites also found them a people of moral abandon. Where whites were austere and puritanical, Mexicans were vulgar; where whites were reserved, Mexicans were unabashed; where whites were conscious of moral principles, Mexicans appeared thoughtless of moral prohibitions. As whites saw it, Mexicans expressed emotions and impulses that ought to be suppressed.

Whenever whites discussed the Mexicans' moral nature, references to sexuality punctuated their remarks. The *fandango*, for instance, was identified with lewd passions and lasciviousness. The erotic nature of this traditional Mexican dance often led to prudish comments from onlookers.[4] *Señoritas* were described as especially sensuous when participating in the dance; accounts conspicuously slighted the lustful nature of their male partners. "Voluptuous and fascinating as the Mexican women are," noted Frederic Benjamin Page, writing of his personal experience in the Republic of Texas, "they are never more so than when excited by soft music and the rapturous *fandango* of which they are so fond. Love then sparkles in their eyes, and their sensitive hearts yield irresistibly to the pleasures which it awakes." The love of the *fandango* was thought to be universal with the Mexican women, and one of the last pleasures they would willingly renounce.[5]

Perhaps in an attempt to further distance themselves from a dance that tended to arouse inner doubts as to their own morality, Anglos generally stated that only certain elements of Hispanic society were attracted to the revelry of the *fandango*. In San Antonio, for example, the educated families, the elite of the city, the better society whom whites likened with themselves, were thought to be in control of their morality. The ones who gathered to enjoy the obscene dance were described as the lowest species of humanity—the poor, the uneducated, the mixed-bloods.[6] George Wilkins Kendall of the *New Orleans Picayune*, attended one of these occasions in San Antonio in 1841 and found it quite disreputable. Keeping time to a cracked violin was a single couple shuffling away using a species of break-down negro step, the newspaperman reported. The woman resembled an Egyptian mummy and her partner was even uglier. A group of slovenly, badly dressed Mexican girls sitting upon benches at either end of the room and an old woman in one corner selling cigars and whiskey completed the company.[7] Such was the vulgarity that distinguished the morally defective from the morally pure.

But the *fandango* was only one piece of evidence of the Mexicans' lack of moral fiber that evoked comments from self-righteous whites. A variety of other indications of Mexican immorality also came in for emphasis, especially in the 1840s and 1850s when whites, caught up in the spirit of Manifest Destiny, were reinforcing their image of themselves and the country. According to the several accounts Anglos left, Mexicans were so mindless of moral decency that they thought practically nothing of exhibiting their bodies publicly. Children ran around half-clad and some of the adults also verged on nakedness. Moreover, Mexicans of both sexes seemed unconcerned about such nudity, oblivious to the post-1836 attempts to impose social taboos on the revelation of the flesh. They continued their customary practice of mixed nude bathing in public streams, something that must have confirmed for most whites the moral corruption they imputed to Mexicanos. But at least R. H. Williams, a cattle rancher in Central Texas, recognized the practice for what it was. In 1861 at the Medina River, he came upon a set of Mexican men, women, and children diving, swimming, and splashing each other in a beautiful pool, bathing in the bright sunshine, none wearing more than "nature's garb." Realizing that they were not disturbed by his arrival, he joined them. Then, manifesting a more profound grasp of cultural difference than his Anglo compatriots, he noted, "I never saw a merrier bathing party, or a more innocent one."[8]

Most whites were less understanding; indeed reactions were often dramatically different, for many responded to similar scenes with astonishment if not shock. An anonymous visitor to San Antonio in 1837 thought Mexicans to have a different understanding from Anglos of the relations between the sexes. "On one occasion when I went to bathe I found a male and a female at the place which is usually resorted to for such purposes, which led me to withdraw." The prospective swimmer felt satisfied that his assertion concerning the difference in moral and sexual conduct was justified when the Mexican male reassured him that his presence would lead to no complications should he join in the "promiscuous" association.[9] The German geologist Ferdinand Roemer, journeying in Texas in the mid-forties, similarly described a startling spectacle from above a certain bridge in the heart of San Antonio: Mexican women and girls bathing in entire nudity, laughing and chattering, showing their agility and skill. Seeming unconcerned about the presence of onlookers, at times they were carried by the current very near the spectators, at which point they would dive and re-emerge some distance away. "If this was done to hide themselves from our view, it was the wrong thing to do," explained the observer, "for the water was so clear that one could see the smallest pebble at the bottom. My companion informed me that this spectacle was repeated daily and that both sexes of the Mexican population were fond of bathing."[10] From his home in the same city in 1847, the French Roman Catholic missionary Emanuel Domenech had an unobscured view of a nearby stream of clear water where women bathed publicly. "The window was in view of all their gambolings," Abbé Domenech reported. "I was therefore obliged to keep it closed during the day." Like the modest clergyman, white San Antonians reacted with embarrassment (if not intolerance). Canvas-covered bathhouses were erected once the Alamo City went through the process of anglicization, much to the perplexity of Tejanos.[11]

The unabashed nudity and other "libertine" manifestations of Tejano culture led to a fantasizing of Mexicans as erotic, sensuous, and voluptuous. When Anglos used Mexicans as counter images to measure their own moral standard—especially where it concerned sexuality—Mexicans appeared less civilized. The anonymous San Antonio visitor of 1837, for example, reported "less reserve and propriety in the manners and conduct of the different sexes in their intercourse with each other than would be tolerated in the States."[12]

The image of Mexicans as irresponsible and promiscuous laid the foundation for another important theme in nineteenth-century Texas—the sexual desire of white men for Mexican women. White men took Mexican *señoritas* to bed, perhaps more often than can ever be known. But the sexual relations were not just something that naturally came to be; on the contrary, they occurred only after the physical drive of white men wrestled with the discriminating psyche that resisted such relations.

As Anglos dispersed throughout those sections of the state where Tejanos lived, or passed through them as travelers, they reported sexual impressions similar to those that early arrivals in the Béxar region had expressed before the Revolution: namely, that *señoritas* and *señoras* were attractive and appealing. Not that Anglos were repudiating their deep aversion for Mexicans in general. But, in the 1840s and 1850s there prevailed a demographic disparity between white males and females, even in Central Texas at first and in South and West Texas until after the Civil War. That was the period when white men expressed their strongest sexual appreciation for Mexican women.

To begin with, male observers of Tejano society usually made fewer critical comments about Mexican women than Mexican men. As one of them put it, the contempt Anglos had for Mexicans as a people did not extend to the ladies.[13] Mexican women were said to possess numerous redeeming traits: charm, courtesy, kindness, generosity, and warm-heartedness. Additionally, there was something inviting and seductive about them. They were attractive, handsomely formed, and had beautiful eyes.[14] An 1840 visitor to San Antonio said that *mestizo* women there were "agreeable, handsome and fascinating . . . They dress plain and tastefully, and in a style best calculated to develop the elegant proportion of their persons. Generally poor, they of course wear but few costly jewels, yet with much good sense seem to consider their own natural charms (which border on the volupt[u]ousness) as the richest ornaments that can adorn a woman, and as those surest to attract the notice and secure the attention of the rougher portion of humanity."[15] Olmsted was duly impressed with what he saw, the larger part of Mexican females in Béxar consisting of "black-eyed, olive girls, full of animation of tongue and glance, but sunk in a soft embonpoint, which added a somewhat extreme good-nature to their charms."[16] In short, there was something appealing about *señoritas*, something lending an attraction that might lead to intimate relations between them and white men.

But before white men could consummate their sexual wishes, some rationalization had to be made. After all, almost impenetrable barriers interceded between desire and aversion, between the sexual drive and the fastidious psyche. Were Mexicans not somewhat different, were they not a backward and lethargic people, defective in many ways? Particularly, were they not a race of mongrels, constituted of Indian and Negro blood? There exists at least some indication that Mexican women could be accepted by whites in Texas under certain circumstances—but only if they could approximate the ideal of white beauty.

There was in antebellum Texas a certain segment of the Mexican population, though a rather small one, that more or less approached this excellence. Relations might safely be had with these candidates (although even here there may have been some restraint due to fear of polluting the white race, since intermixture with them would presumably produce "mongrels" as intermixture between Spaniards and Indians did). Isleñas (from the Canary Islands) and women of "Castilian descent," like their male counterparts, were able to assimilate themselves into white society, and such women seemed to be somewhat acceptable to white men.

A number of men showed a favoritism for this type. Francis Latham, for one, was able to strike up a friendship with Mexicans of creole lineage while staying in San Antonio in 1842; and he had nothing but flattering remarks to make about his hosts. He found in them dark beaming eyes whose intense and expressive emotions suggested the "soul of love." Determined to acquaint himself with the Spanish language, he enjoyed every moment of the lessons, especially as they came from the "smiling lips of a Spanish girl, her full, dark, tender eyes beaming on yours, and sparkling with excited emotion." There was indeed, thought Latham, great intensity of feeling, sincerity, and strength of attachment in the earnest expression in the eyes of a Spanish *señorita*. "And if a 'gentleman of family' may be excused for talking about 'love and girls,'" ended Latham passionately, "they really look as if they could *love harder* and more *devotedly* than any other women. However, it may 'all be in the eye,' after all."[17]

Other transients likewise left no doubt as to where their preferences rested when it came to the shades of a woman's color. William McClintock found little attractive about the females of San Antonio, for, though an admirer of brunettes, he said, he had never fancied very deep colors. But "I have seen two or three of castilian extraction, who would be considered handsome in any circle of society, they are generally tall, in form, and shape, yet of faulty proportions, features inclining to acqueline or Grecian, generally the latter, complexion of rich brunette."[18]

As for those who came to settle in the state as single males, they also searched out the lighter-skinned girls of well-to-do families under the pressure of sexual disparities between white men and white women. The case of South Texas is instructive in regard to the role demography played in race relations. In the 1850s, the Americans and foreigners who arrived in the Rio Grande Valley went so far as to form marriage alliances with leading Spanish-Mexican families, who, given the structure of Hispanic society, probably were of light skin or had pretenses to it. Newcomers expressed very little racial hostility toward Hispanic society. In fact, many simply adapted themselves to the existing conditions, accepting the Spanish language, the Catholic religion, and Tejano culture. When the lower portion of South Texas began the transformation into commercial farming in the 1870s and 1880s, however, racial tolerance changed dramatically as the white population increased and the region ceased to be almost totally Mexican. Recent Anglo arrivals treated both the American/Mexican parents and their offspring as Mexicans. Feelings now came to resemble the prejudice that governed Anglo-Mexican relations elsewhere.[19]

If the men who went into South Texas at mid-century found light-skinned girls to marry, they were most fortunate, for the fact was that "Castilian" women were in short supply all over the state. Even had there been more of them, the white skin of the creole-descended *señoritas* did not necessarily mean automatic acceptance by Texas society. Robert Weakley Brahan, a recent arrival in San Antonio in the 1850s, observed that in Béxar only four or five of the "bloods of Castile" were received into the circles of the elite.[20]

Clearly, most whites had a problem: if they desired to have relations with the native women, it would have to be with partners of a darker hue, women who were part of a culture group which white racial lore considered "mongrel." Whites hardly rushed into marriage with Mexican *señoritas* in the 1820s, even when the Coahuila-Texas state colonization law of 1825 offered free land to Anglos involved in such arrangements. Manifestly, there were obstacles to be overcome.

One such obstacle was, of course, the common white perception of Mexicans as a people afflicted with defective morality. A. B. Lawrence thought they lacked the high moral fabric necessary to preserve them from degrading vices. "Their morals are low," he was sure, "debased in every respect, and licentiousness is scarcely thought worthy of rebuke."[21] Brahan found no houses of ill fame in mid-century Béxar, "but many of these 'greasers' of fine figures and good features, the color of a mulatto, are kept by votaries of sensuability."[22]

As has been seen, Mexican attitudes toward nudity were misunderstood by Anglos, and Mexican styles of dress did not always conform to Anglo notions of propriety. To Anglos, Mexican women seemed to take a carefree attitude toward their persons that went some way in confirming the fantasy of Mexican moral defectiveness. Wherever travelers went in the antebellum period, they noted more or less the same thing. Mexican women made only token efforts (with *rebozos* and the like) to hide their bodies; they hardly succeeded in their attempts; and they exposed their breasts without even a blush.[23] According to Olmsted, they dressed frequently in nothing more than a chemise, "as low as possible in the neck, sometimes even lower," and calico petticoat. "Their dresses seemed lazily reluctant to cover their plump persons, and their attitudes were always expressive of the influence of Southern sun upon national manners."[24] Down in Brownsville, Benjamin McIntyre soon became thoroughly disgusted with the environs. "I am sick of the sights that I daily meet with . . . bare breasted women, naked children . . ." But some time later, the Union soldier entered into his diary that he missed "many things which once was pasttime and interest to me

. . . [including] the half nude women sitting at the street corner with their basket of oranges."[25]

A principal Anglo explanation of Mexicanas' willingness to expose themselves was that they were bereft of ideas of morality, or, perhaps, were especially passionate. Of those attributing special sexual ardency to Mexican women, none was more emphatic than Olmsted. "The constancy of the married women was made very light of," he argued, "not that their favors were purchasable, but that they are sometimes seized by a strong penchant for some other than their lord."[26]

A convenient result (and perhaps also a cause) of the idea of Mexican voluptuousness and of the passionate (though not necessarily lascivious) Mexican woman longing for sexual contact was that it provided white men with a pretext for associating with the females of a people who were racially unacceptable and considered, in general, with disdain and abhorrence. There are demonstrable incongruities between the liberal association of Anglos with Mexican *señoritas*, so much different from their ideal of perfect womanhood, and the racial overtones in their killing of Mexican men. How did white men rationalize this inconsistent behavior?

Nineteenth-century Texas history provides numerous accounts (by white men) suggesting that Mexican women, either single or married, were promiscuous—especially with white men. Olmsted, for example, asserted that "There was testimony of [promiscuity] in the various shades and features of their children; in fact, we thought the number of babies of European hair and feature exceeded the native olive in number."[27] He was not alone in this conviction. The adventurer John C. Duval, who had escaped the Goliad massacre, was convinced that obliging *señoritas* preferred "the blue-eyed fair complexioned young Saxons to their copper-colored beaux."[28] John Reid also deduced from various sources, including hearsay and observation, that Anglo males were held in high estimation by Mexican females.[29] It was the case in nineteenth-century Texas that white men made a serendipitous discovery: Mexican women lusted for them!

Thus, the position of the white men was that they had been lured across the racial line. Fornication could be justified on the pretense that it was caused by Mexican women having a penchant for them. Contempt for *all* Mexicans, including "greaser women," and austere mores and taboos prohibiting intercourse with "mongrels," could then be overcome. The theme of the sexually ardent woman yearning for their attentions provided a fortuitous rationale for having relations with members of a race they otherwise considered so contemptible. If Mexican women craved their intimacy, it was inevitable that they should yield to the urges of nature.

Once this rationalization appeased the mind, many Anglo men went ahead and married Mexicans.[30] Others simply lived with them. George W. B. Evans, passing through the Cibolo Creek area on his way to California gold in 1849, found one American woman promiscuously living among several men, the other families consisting of white men with Mexican women.[31] When Albert Richardson passed through El Paso in the late 1850s, he found only a very few American ladies; most of the white men kept Mexican mistresses.[32] The rest of the story, obviously, is too intimate to be known. But judging from attitudes expressed toward women, it is almost certain that many Anglo males consummated their fantasies clandestinely.

Up to 1860, then, Anglos probed the intimate nature of Tejano sexuality just as they examined the biological and cultural make-up of Mexicans. Obviously that inspection had something to do with natural curiosity as well as the desire to make moral comparisons, but it also corresponded to the fact that, on numerous occasions, white men had little access to white women. Furthermore, they may also have been cross-culturally applying notions about lascivious black women,[33] since this was the era when the images Anglos conjured up about Mexicans were certainly affected by previous experiences with colored peoples east of the Sabine River.

In the same way that the changes brought about by the Civil War and Reconstruction affected the emphasis whites placed on some of their other attitudes toward Mexicanos, so did they bring about a de-emphasis on Anglo perceptions of Mexican morality and sexuality. Writers no longer allotted the same space to previous motifs—travelers, in particular, hardly made reference to them. The nudity which had embarrassed so many earlier itinerants (but attracted them also), for example, was now hardly mentioned. The native Texans themselves were not greatly preoccupied with Mexican morality. In fact, by the 1890s the image of the immoral Mexican was the subject of reference only infrequently.

When the topic did come up, Texans mostly repeated old themes. The *fandango*, for example, still came in for condemnation, for it remained an open reminder of Mexican vulgarity. Thus did the *Brownsville Ranchero* in 1868 opine that Mexican "*pelados*" had degraded it from its original state into "pandemonium." Once a sort of half-jig, half-ballet, danced gracefully to the tune of a guitar or flute and relished for its graceful motions and varied steps, the *Ranchero* said, the dance now attracted the outcasts of society. *Fan-*

dangos were an evil practice, continued the *Ranchero*, a relic of barbarism, and a school for immorality. Obscene language and foul imprecations filled the atmosphere. Gambling, horse racing, robbery, theft, maiming, prostitution, murder, and drunkenness flourished. Jealousies and rivalries engendered by the corruptness of some of the women led inevitably to the stimulation of more vicious passions, for it was seldom that the spilling of human blood at *fandangos* was not done "at the instigation of some outcast of society in woman shape."[34] Similarly, the *San Antonio Express* of 1874 editorialized that so much profit derived from running *fandangos* that proprietors actually paid transportation of the "painted Jezebels" to and from the place of entertainment. Those attending such occasions included citizens of respectable standing.[35]

As could have been expected, several cities called for the termination of the dance and the occasions during which it was practiced. The *Brownsville Ranchero*, following on its criticism of the *fandango*, called for a city ordinance to banish this "barbarian entertainment."[36] In San Antonio, likewise, a local paper in 1872 reminded the town's good citizens that the *fandangos* being held weekly west of the San Pedro Creek had been declared illegal in the city.[37] In Austin, Mayor T. B. Wheeler in 1874 commended his city council for passing an ordinance suppressing the *fandango*. The measure, Mayor Wheeler asserted, was having good effect toward restoring peace and quiet to that portion of the city formerly disturbed by "those disgraceful and demoralizing assemblages."[38] By the late 1870s, however, *fandangos* had ceased to attract public attention, though Tejanos continued holding them surreptitiously.

At the same time, bawdy houses provided an opportunity for Anglos to lapse from propriety without thinking themselves responsible for the transgression. In 1879, Hans Mickle, the wandering *San Antonio Express* correspondent, selected the area west of the San Pedro Creek in San Antonio for part of his wanderings. Since large numbers of Mexicans lived there, and the prevailing general impression was that everything in the section was of a questionable character, he thought the *barrio* would be of great interest to his Anglo readers. Employing Deputy City Marshall Jesús Cárdenas as his guide, the reporter headed westward. After some walking and description of *tamale* vendors and gambling halls, Mickle came upon San Antonio's "Five Points," the history of which he said would fill volumes. Known locally as the "coral," it was a collection of *jacales* situated in the center of a block where "women of the very lowest type" could be found, including whites and blacks in addition to

Mexicans. Continuing his venture through "Chihuahua" (the Mexican barrio) in search of wicked places, he headed south on Laredo Street, passing several dives and places of low respectability. Determined to see firsthand the "abode of the demi-monde," he visited the three most prominent houses west of the San Pedro. In sumptuously furnished rooms, respectable men of the city and men of the cloth mingled with "fine matronly women of intelligent countenances, with some who showed unmistakenly that their's had been a life of riot and dissipation, and with others whose faces could transfer to a church sociable."

This social evil, remarked Mickle, existing in every city of the world despite all attempts to eradicate it, was not necessarily confined to San Antonio's Mexican quarter.[39] He did not explain why he had specifically chosen "Chihuahua" as the object of his survey. Considering that Mexicans were thought of as lacking morality and self-control, it no doubt seemed natural to whites to identify Mexican sections of urban areas with vice, licentiousness, and moral degradation.

Clearly, whites still clung to their image of Mexicans as a people with an aberrant sense of morality. According to other allegations, Mexicans were totally oblivious of the criminality of rape and looked upon adultery as almost legitimate.[40] The prominent citizens of San Angelo told J. E. MacGowan, a *Chattanooga Times* correspondent, that Mexicans had no particular morals concerning sexual relations, "except that mothers try hard to guard their daughters until marriage, or at least to the time of betrothal. Changing wives is not uncommon and neither partner has much regard for the proprieties when living together."[41] At least one local resident, signing himself "Adios," took issue with the above contention. Mexicans were not wholly immoral, he argued, though admittedly they did not "look upon a lapse of virtue with that holy horror which our uncontaminated race does."[42] And Lee C. Harby, the *Harper's New Monthly Magazine* journalist, writing about Mexicans of a border town, proclaimed: "Be it known that these people are not a moral one, and a family of Mexican children may vary in all shades between black and white."[43]

Most of what was said about the more intimate aspects of sexuality in the postwar period was simply a rehash of earlier views. Whites already knew all there was to know about Mexican voluptuousness and there was nothing novel to report. *Señoritas* were still attractive and appealing; according to the enduring lore, they retained their passionate countenances.[44] Further, persistent fantasy

held, these women looked toward white men with the same estimation as always. Though the idea of Mexican women yearning for
them was so prosaic as to merit little public expression, once in a
while something appeared in print revealing the white men's latent
convictions. The following fantastic account of an American's adventure with a Mexican girl in Parral, Chihuahua, found its way into
the columns of a number of newspapers in the state:

> The *Señoritas* have but a faint idea of kissing, that art from
> which so few possess the capacity of extracting the most avail-
> able ecstasy—and I one day offered to show a dark eyed, raven-
> haired young lady how *los Americanos* performed the art. She
> laughingly agreed—it is unnecessary for me to say that the
> male members and duenna were out of the way—and I ad-
> vanced upon the adventure; my left arm encircled her waist,
> extending over the right shoulder downward; my right arm
> bent at the elbow, afforded my hand an opportunity of accom-
> modating her dimpled chin. Gently folding back her head and
> throwing a look, or rather a rapid series of looks of unutterable
> nothings into my eyes, I gazed clean through her's for a long
> breath I tapped her lips. It was a revelation to her; she quivered
> visibly, but, instead of returning my kiss, she broke away from
> my embrace and went off to lock her self up, frightened,
> pleased, but astounded. I was satisfied that I had done myself
> and country proud, although, to be candid, it was merely a me-
> chanical operation with me, done for the sake of effect, as I did
> not really care for the girl. I think she remained in maiden
> meditation for two days, but at last I saw her, and she told me,
> with a deep blush, that she wished she had been born in Amer-
> ica, to be kissed like that.[45]

The story's wide dissemination probably had little to do with a journalistic commitment to reporting the news of one man's affair
(whether real or concocted) with a woman who found Americans irresistible. One can imagine newspaper editors seeing in it proof of
what society believed—that white men were irresistible to Mexicanas—not to mention the public's relish for a good story, especially
one of a salacious nature.

Thus, as in the old times, whites could be enticed across the
barriers of Anglo moral decency. Along the border regions, especially, where the demography of the 1870s and 1880s resembled that
of Central Texas in the 1840s and 1850s, interracial mixing was

common. At Fort McIntosh, for example, the soldiers frequently drew upon "black-eyed dark-skinned *señoritas*" for company.[46] In Fort Davis the same situation existed, and a resident reported: "In the absence of the fair ones of their own nationality the young men proudly pay their addresses to the charming daughters of our sister Republic who reside here." They believed it best

> to make love to the lips that are nearest
> When away from the ones that they love.[47]

Quite obviously, whites still took Mexicanas to bed in the postbellum period. The many mixed couples that took marriage vows in the last three decades of the century attest to continued interracial sex;[48] presumably, illicit relations continued as well. There were clearly moments when the private passions of white males could override their more belligerent attitudes toward "greasers."

While Texan society never really condoned this sort of interracial union, at the same time the tensions that were part of black/white sexual mixing were not evidenced. Texas did not pass anti-miscegenation laws preventing Anglo-Mexican marriages, but the recurring specification that such marriages were with "Spanish" women[49] is suggestive of the disapproving attitudes that did pervade the state. White men were even known to get into fights over Tejanas, not only with Mexican men, but with other Anglos as well. This would have been unthinkable where black women were involved. In the racial categorization that existed in the state, Mexicans apparently stood in the middle, affected only partially by the taboos that applied to sexual relations between whites and peoples considered to be darker than Mexicans.

5. Disloyalty and Subversion

Contrary to what whites expected (and desired) of an indolent and immoral people, Tejanos did not quiescently conform to the passive image Anglos had created for them. Instead, Tejanos annoyingly meddled in institutional things, following a historical path which frequently collided with what whites regarded as genuinely American. Subscribing firmly to ideals of American democracy, Mexicans provoked whites into questioning their sentiments and loyalty. By taking issue with Texans who advocated one thing but practiced the opposite, they found themselves in the ironic position of being considered un-American.

The question of Tejano patriotism came up often. During the Texas Revolution of 1836, Anglos suspected Mexicanos of siding with Santa Anna, even as some rendered important service to the insurrectionary cause.[1] Following independence, similar concerns were focused on Tejano attitudes toward slavery—an institution which had never settled well with the Mexicans in Texas. From the beginning, they had looked for ways to undermine or sabotage it, and the increase in runaway slaves immediately following independence attested to the degree of Mexican sympathy toward slaves and the aid Tejanos extended in inducing them to escape into Mexico. This practice became so widespread that it led to talk of stationing Rangers along the Rio Grande.[2] The itinerant Olmsted heard Texans complaining of Mexicans tampering with slave property, consorting with blacks, and "making no distinction from pride of race."[3] According to the *Texas State Gazette*, Mexicans placed themselves on an equal level with slaves and stirred up among them a spirit of insubordination.[4] They were subverting the institution that stood at the foundation of Southern society.

Moreover, Mexicans did not stop at fraternizing with slaves. Using their status as free men to advantage, they successfully rescued a number of them from bondage and transported them to freedom in Mexico. Through the sparsely settled, semidesert frontier between Central Texas and the Rio Grande, Mexicanos risked the peril of apprehension and punishment for violating the slave codes. At a time when Southern slave masters were suspicious of any nonconformer, Mexicanos upheld their principles and, as a result, were denounced by Anglo Texans as rascals with no claim to respectability and no knowledge of civilized politics. Anglos depicted Mexicans as reprobates, transient peons, or individuals with no permanent interests or attachments to Texas soil and institutions. Citizens of the town of Seguin referred to them in resolutions as "a vagrant class, a lazy, thievish, horde of lazaron [*lázaros*, beggars] who in many instances are fugitives from justice in Mexico, highway robbers, horses and cattle thieves, and idle vagabonds, who prowl about our western country with little visible occupation or pursuit."[5]

There were certain Mexicanos who might qualify as candidates for acceptance as good and loyal Americans, however. When Rodrigo Hinojosa captured two runaway slaves in Rio Grande City in 1860, whites lavished unrestrained praise on his efforts. "The prompt action of the Mexicans in restoring the fugitives to their owners, is deserving of merited praise," wrote the *Corpus Christi Ranchero*. "All must admit that some of our Mexican population are of service to the community at large, as well as being law-abiding citizens."[6] In November of that year, when a runaway slave crossed into Nuevo Laredo, a future Confederate hero named Santos Benavides went into Mexico and retrieved him. According to Michael Lidwell, from Benavides' home town of Laredo, it was not the first time that Don Santos had distinguished himself in restoring runaways to their owners. He had ever been "foremost in confronting danger in support of the laws and institutions of Texas," and despite that danger, he had always refused recompense for his exertions. "The above facts, when known to the people of Texas," continued Lidwell, would "go far toward opening the eyes of many to the erroneous impression so generally entertained regarding the portion of our fellow-citizens of Mexican origin."[7]

To plantation owners in Central Texas and their supporters, however, nothing short of decisive action against the Mexican saboteurs would do. Early in September 1854 the white citizenry of Seguin passed resolutions prohibiting Mexican "peons" from entering Guadalupe County because of their alleged sympathy with the bondspeople. Further, measures were to be taken against anyone found trading or communicating with slaves without permission of their owners. A standing committee of "twenty discreet men" was to enforce the resolutions. Should the law not act promptly to protect the institution of slavery, editorialized the *Texas State Gazette*, then the citizens of Guadalupe County would take it upon themselves to correct the abuses as a matter of self-preservation.[8]

In Bexar County, some reacted to the problem similarly. A writer in the *San Antonio Ledger* early in 1855 suggested that Mexican strangers coming into the city register at the mayor's office and give an account of themselves and their business. Any Mexican who was unknown to any respectable resident of San Antonio and unable to produce a satisfactory certificate, continued the writer, would be required to leave the city premises immediately.[9]

Delegates from several counties west of the Colorado River met in a convention at Gonzales in October 1854. Their purpose, in view of the continued jeopardy to their human property, was to devise remedies vis-à-vis the evil of black-Mexican association and to adopt stern measures directed at preventing slave stealing. The convention resolved that counties should organize vigilance committees to prosecute persons tampering with slaves and that all citizens and slaveholders were to work diligently to prohibit Mexicans from contacting blacks. When Olmsted journeyed through the area, whites still retained a strong suspicion of the Mexican population and continued to drive them out at the least provocation.[10]

In Austin, where a citizens' committee accused Mexican residents of horse theft and exiled twenty families from their homes into the western counties in the spring of 1853,[11] similar attitudes prevailed. Through resolutions, Austin citizens decreed that all transient Mexicans should be warned to leave within ten days; that all remaining should be forcibly expelled unless their good character and good behavior were substantiated by responsible American citizens; that Mexicans should no longer be employed and their presence in the area should be discouraged; and that a committee of "ten energetic gentlemen" should be appointed to carry out these resolutions.[12] By late October, the Vigilante Committee had discharged its duties: no Mexicans remained in the city unvouched for. "It should be the duty of every citizen to aid in preserving the present state of things," a local paper recommended.[13] In 1855, some families returned but were once again expelled.[14] Olmsted appraised the situation a short time later:

Wherever slavery in Texas has been carried in a wholesale way, into the neighborhood of Mexicans, it has been found necessary to treat them as outlaws. Guaranteed, by the Treaty of Guadalupe Hidalgo, equal rights with all other citizens of the United States and of Texas, the whole native population of county after county has been driven, by the formal proceedings of substantial planters, from its homes, and forbidden, on pain of no less punishment than instant death, to return to the vicinity of the plantations.[15]

Bringing further reaction and casting doubt upon the Mexicans' loyalty was a slave plot discovered in September 1856. According to a committee of investigation appointed by aroused Colorado County citizens, a well-organized insurrection to overthrow the established order was planned, and among the leaders was a Mexican known only as Frank. Every Mexican in the county was suspected of being party to the conspiracy, on the premise that Mexicans had long been acting as incendiaries wherever slavery existed; there was apparently no other evidence against them. From what the committee gathered, the insurrection was planned for September 6, 1856, when, at a late hour of the night, slaves in concert with the Mexicans were to make a desperate effort for freedom. With passwords adopted, two to ten slaves were to be apportioned per house; then, armed with pistols, bowie knives, and guns, they were to murder the entire white population "with the exception of the young ladies, who were to be taken captives, and made the wives of the diabolical murderers of their parents and friends." Once this was accomplished, blacks were to plunder their owners' homes, take their horses and arms, and fight their way to Mexico with the aid of the Mexicans, determined to "leave not a shadow behind." When whites discovered the plans, all Mexicans in the county were arrested and ordered to leave within five days. A resolution was adopted unanimously "forever forbidding any Mexican from coming within the limits of the county." As for the blacks, three of the ringleaders were hung, two hundred lashed, and two whipped to death. A well-organized patrol was established to prevent further occurrences.[16]

In other areas, also, Mexicans came in for suspicion on account of their stand against slavery during the latter 1850s. In Matagorda County, all Mexicans were expelled on the pretext that they were vagrant, lower-class peons who "have no fixed domicile, but hang around the plantations, taking the likeliest negro girls for wives . . . they often steal horses, and these girls, too, and endeavor to run them to Mexico." Expulsion was described as "a mild course" by whites who would have felt justified in resorting to "lynch law."[17] In the next year, Uvalde County passed resolutions prohibiting all Mexicans from traversing the area unless they had in their possession a passport granted by some white authority.[18]

Other political trends during the 1850s also bore upon Tejanos vexatiously. The upstart Native American Party (often called the Know-Nothings) demanded that they demonstrate their nationalistic sentiments by accepting its superpatriotic philosophy of "America for and by Americans" and its demands for limitation of immigration, imposition of sterner restrictions on naturalization, and the curtailment of the feared aggression and corrupting tendency of the Roman Catholic Church. Not surprisingly, Mexicanos adamantly opposed the Know-Nothing principles. In Bexar County, they rejected the American Party almost unanimously; in Hidalgo County and other Rio Grande border areas, they also registered their disapproval in 1856.[19]

The Know-Nothings were infuriated by the "treasonous" implications of the San Antonio election. They denounced Bexareños as "ignorant, vicious, besotted greasers." Incapable of determining political advantages and disadvantages for themselves, editorialized the party's news organ, the *Austin State Times*, the "deluded horde of Mexican peons" had fallen under the influence of the priesthood. By threatening excommunication or denial of the sacraments, clergymen had persuaded Tejanos to vote against their inclinations, the paper claimed.[20]

The Juan Cortina insurgency, which followed closely on the heels of the many trying events that taxed the American temperament in the fifties, further placed Tejanos in the class of suspicious citizens in 1859 and 1860. This was an expression of the smoldering discontent prevailing in southern Texas since Anglo-Americans had inversed the social, economic, and political order. In the years during the Mexican War and continuing into the 1850s, Anglos and Europeans had drifted into the Rio Grande Valley and had used their ties with influential people in Austin, their knowledge of the new political system, their connection with well-to-do families in South Texas, and their advantage as conquerors to assume a dominant role in the affairs of the section. Cortina's movement, then, called attention to a government that had deviated from the democratic principles it espoused. In this respect, the rebellion was similar to Shays' Rebellion, the Whiskey Rebellion, and the Texas Revolution. As whites came to see it, however, it signified the ungrateful nature of Mexicanos who knew little of civilized life and did not appreciate the perquisites of a democratic society.

The immediate catalyst for the insurgency was an incident that occurred in a Brownsville café on July 13, 1859, in which Cortina, responding to an ethnic epithet from the Anglo sheriff, shot the lawman and retreated to his mother's ranch nearby. In late September, Cortina occupied Brownsville with a sizable force of followers and freed some prisoners in the city jail. After being persuaded to leave, he crossed into Mexico, but returned to the Texas side in mid-October when news reached him that one of his men had been jailed in Brownsville. Seeing Cortina as a threat to the city and the region, Anglo citizens organized into military units and, along with militia elements from Matamoros, launched several attacks on Cortina's stronghold at his mother's Rancho del Carmen, all of which Cortina repulsed. Other efforts to dislodge him were unsuccessful, Cortina's victories making him a hero in the eyes of fellow Mexicanos and inspiring many to join his ranks. Not until mid-December did the federal military succeed in pushing him upriver and into Mexico.

While at Rancho del Carmen, Cortina had issued several proclamations of grievances, which in light of history, could hardly be challenged as to veracity. He accused whites of despoiling Mexicanos of their land, of prosecuting and robbing the native element for no other crime than that of being of Mexican origin. Since 1848, he grieved, "flocks of vampires, in the guise of men, came and scattered themselves in the settlements, without any capital except the corrupt heart and the most perverse intentions," robbing the natives of their land titles and property, hunting them down, incarcerating and murdering them.[21] Cortina's constant argument remained that he had simply acted in behalf of a downtrodden people. Indeed, according to one of his proclamations, Cortina and his followers hoped that Governor-elect Sam Houston would give them legal protection.[22]

But so far as whites were concerned, Mexicans had no right to protection by the state. The *Brownsville Flag*, for example, specifically denied them the privilege of dissent, arguing that Mexicanos were without legal title to citizenship. The United States Supreme Court, contended the *Flag*, had decided in *McKinney v. Saviego* (1855) that Article VIII of the Treaty of Guadalupe Hidalgo had made no reference to Texas, and consequently citizenship had not accrued to Mexican residents of the state. Their "adherence to the common enemy" had rendered them ineligible for citizenship according to fundamental law.[23] Thus, Anglos in the Valley considered Cortina and his followers to be connected to Mexican disorder rather than American order, as can be seen in their descriptions of them. The most dangerous segment of the Mexican population, *pelados* from the towns and ranches along the Rio Grande, allegedly comprised Cortina's ranks.[24] According to Major Samuel P. Heintzelman, who was sent to reconnoiter for the federal government, the class of people who joined Cortina were thriftless and vicious and lived principally on jerked beef and corn, or *frijoles* (beans) for luxury.[25] The *Corpus Christi Ranchero* further characterized them as an idle, depraved, thievish, ignorant, and fanatical population, as fugitive peons from the interior of Mexico and escaped felons from that country as well as Texas.[26]

When the Civil War broke out, many Texas-Mexicans refused to give their allegiance to the Confederacy. After all, they had been actively undermining slavery. The Tejano community was not unanimous in its support of the Stars and Stripes; in fact, more Tejanos served in the Confederate ranks than in the Union forces.[27] But enough of them disputed the southern cause to rouse Anglos into questioning their loyalty. In Brownsville, for example, the Confederate officer Hamilton P. Bee reported that Mexicanos could not be trusted and that, if the town fell to the northern forces, *guerrilleros* would immediately flock to the Union units. Bee advised a peaceful attitude toward the natives to prevent "a large and effective force of a race embittered against us by real or imaginary wrongs."[28]

Naturally, those who lent their support to the Union cause incurred the censure of irate Confederates. Among these were Mexicanos in Zapata County who in April 1861 vowed that they would not take the oath of allegiance to the state or Confederacy and that they would not obey or respect the authorities holding office under either, but would remain loyal to the government of the United States. Organizing themselves into an army of forty to eighty men, they headed for Carrizo, the county seat, intending to keep Precinct No. 3 county officers from taking the oath of office prescribed by the Secession Convention and threatening at the same time to take the public funds of the tax assessor and collector. Confederate forces attacked the dissenters at Rancho Clareño, below Carrizo, and there defeated them on April 15, killing several Mexicans, including the two leaders. The *Corpus Christi Ranchero* denounced the Mexicans. "What is the cause of this trouble? Pronunciamientos and taking up arms against our country constitute treason, which is a crime punishable with death," warned the paper. "Those who thus offend may rest assured that, sooner or later, they will get the reward of their deeds. The curse of God be with ye!" The raid was described subsequently by the Mexican Border Commission, sent by Mexico to investigate border violence in 1873, as one in which several in-offensive inhabitants were assassinated by the Confederates.[29]

Tejano Union resistance against the Texas Confederates con-tinued throughout the war, primarily in South Texas, where Tejanos harassed Confederate troops and seized cotton and stock for Union forces. That activity further enhanced the image of the Mexican as an unappreciative wretch; and in fact, some Texans referred to the Rio Grande forces in 1863 as "bands of abolitionists, outlaws, Mex-icans and fugitive negroes." John Salmon "Rip" Ford, commander of the Rio Grande Military District, described the abolitionist move-ment as one of brutal men motivated by base passions and led by those whose career had been marked by treason, assassination, and robbery.[30] Those Tejanos who remained true to the Confederacy, on the other hand, earned kudos for their loyalty.[31] Ironically, what they were really being praised for was helping to "keep the niggers in their place."

After the war, while ex-Confederates did all they could to sub-vert Republican rule in the state, many Tejanos persisted in their Union sentiment and sympathized with Radical Reconstruction. Most of the Mexicanos of El Paso, for example, remained opposed to the Democratic Party and loyal to the Reconstruction governments. A correspondent for the *New York Times* sent to Texas with instruc-tions to look into the testimony given before the Reconstruction Committee—to the effect that the state remained unreconciled to the northern victory—similarly reported that the twenty thousand Mexicans in the state were loyal to Union rule. According to the re-port, the allegiance of the Mexicans could not be doubted.[32]

The fact of the matter was, however, that there was an element in Hispanic society which either had southern sympathies or was neutral. Moreover, unlike ex-Confederates, most Mexicans were not disfranchised by the provisions of Congressional Reconstruction. Under such circumstances, conservatives were willing to recognize at least some Tejanos as "real Americans" and to plead for their sup-port. In Cameron County, an ex-Confederate "freeborn white cit-izen," seeking to enlist the Mexicans' favor for the conservative element, urged them to register, and vote against the Radicals. Mex-icans, he asserted, were now in a situation where they could choose between "confiscation, negro equality and their ultimate extinction, and on the other hand liberty, rights of interest and social distinc-tion; choose between self-government and the yoke of military op-pression; choose between excessive taxation and free trade; choose between life and death."[33] At the same time, the *Brownsville Ranchero* indignantly denounced a certain document in circulation as a "politically striped pig of radicalism" which likewise appealed to the Mexican vote. The paper censured the Radicals for attempts to woo the Mexican voter into their ranks with promises so "grandiloquent as to cause every Mexican green-horn to drop his *tortilla*, go back on his *tamales*, sell out his *chile con carne*, kick his *frijoles* to the devil and gapingly stand ready to receive the newly found bread and manna, and milk and honey to be dished up in pursuance to this radical Mexican bill of fare."[34]

In San Antonio, where Mexicanos comprised a significant proportion of the electorate, similar appeals were made. There the ex-Confederate Democrats could rely on old Hispanics, who, having penetrated white society, wielded enough power among Mexicans to make political contests quite competitive. Moreover, the platform of the conservatives could be amplified to attract the Mexican component of the city. As the *San Antonio Herald* articulated it, American, German, Irish, French, and Mexican citizens of the state should unite in forming a white man's party. "White, not black, must rule," it emphasized.[35]

Among those campaigning in behalf of Democratic conservatism in San Antonio were families like the Yturris, Ruizes, and Navarros. A signer of the Texas Declaration of Independence from Mexico, José Antonio Navarro, was a member of the Conservative Party's Executive Committee that addressed voters of Bexar, Wilson, Kerr, and other South Texas counties in February 1868 on the "supremacy of the white race and the peace and happiness of ourselves, our wives and children." A committee circular asked: "Shall negro Supremacy be embodied as a portion of the organic law of the State? Should white men stand below the negro in the ranks of freemen?" The circular opposed black supremacy and the degradation of the white race.[36]

The Radicals in San Antonio included individuals such as E. Mondragón and J. M. Chávez. Through their news organ, *El Mexicano de Tejas*, the men of this faction advocated Afro-American equality. They adhered to the general Radical Republican philosophy which advocated suffrage without distinction of race or color, and reproached, alongside Anglo Radicals, the conservative attempt in San Antonio to form a white man's party with the assistance of the privileged Mexican population.[37]

In the 1870s and after, political corruption was as common in Texas as in other parts of the country, with Texas Anglos using Mexicanos to further their own interests just as northern politicians used European immigrants. Though such practices fell outside American constitutional provisions, by a peculiar twist of logic, it was not Anglos who were considered un-American for employing such mechanisms, but Tejanos for allegedly allowing Anglos to manipulate them.

According to critics of the practice, a common scenario unfolded at voting time: illiterate and ignorant Mexicans were rounded up on the eve of an election, taken to some deserted house or barn or herded into corrals, and there supplied with plenty of whiskey and rations. The next morning they would be marched to the polls, their tickets filled out, then voted by companies, platoons, and squads, and quickly released.[38] As the *El Paso Herald*, a Republican organ, described the practice in April 1890:

> Last night the democrats following out their old time custom, gathered as many Mexicans as they could in various parts of the city. They had music and beer galore, and as the swarthy degenerate sons of ancient Spain poured the beer down their throats, the Democratic Healers poured unadulterated democracy in their ears. The largest corral was in the Schutz building on San Francisco Street opposite the Bullion office. Here there was congregated full 250 or 300 Mexicans in various stages and conditions of drunkenness. The entire neighborhood for blocks around were disturbed during the night by the howls, screams, and blasphemy of the motley crowd. Early this morning when the polls were opened the inmates of the corral were held back by Ed Fink who stood in the door pushing them back and sorting them out to others who in turn drove them to the polls.[39]

In the border regions, the newspapers reported, Mexican Americans crossed the Rio Grande, recruited and paid voters, and imported them on election days with orders to cast their ballot for the chosen candidates.[40] Other accounts said Mexicans were carried to the county clerk, who, for the modest sum of twenty-five cents per head, declared them citizens. Thence they would be herded into corrals and voted.[41]

Actually, Mexican American political participation during the period was more complex,[42] but blame for deviating from democratic norms fell on them nonetheless. Anglos attempted to correct such practices, not by seeking to curb the influence of the power brokers, but by attempting to disfranchise Mexicans. Beeville citizens, for instance, in 1899 called upon the legislature to submit to the people a state constitutional amendment making the poll tax a prerequisite for voting. They also suggested that election laws be amended so that no man would be permitted to vote unless he was a citizen of the United States.[43]

One reason why Anglos felt Tejanos ought not to be trusted with the ballot, many observers maintained, was that Tejanos made no effort to assimilate; they identified with customs and causes that were Mexican instead of those of their adopted country. What particularly disturbed Anglos was the Mexicans' retention of the Spanish language and their refusal to learn English. In the Rio Grande Valley, when Spanish-speakers were called upon to serve on county and city juries, noted a journalist, an interpreter had to translate the evidence, the charge of the judge, and all proceedings. Officers of the law could not read or write English in some of those towns, noted another.[44]

Almost all who witnessed this tendency rebuked it and judged it un-American. "It is incumbent upon all foreigners when they come in the country to cultivate and speak the English language and teach it in their public schools to the exclusion of all others," opined a correspondent for the *San Antonio Express* upon passing through San Diego, Texas, where English and Spanish both were taught.[45] Brownsville Mexicans' adherence to the Spanish language might be laudable in the abstract as evincing a love of their native land, wrote local historian W. H. Chatfield in the early 1890s, but it was not commendable considering that they lived in an American town under the protection of the laws of the United States.[46] In San Angelo, the "sensation of the hour" during the Tom Green County Democratic Convention of 1886 turned out to be the expulsion of a large delegation of Mexicans when Captain J. R. Nasworthy proposed that "no party be allowed to vote in the convention who cannot speak the United States language." The resolution was carried out amid great applause.[47]

Quite obviously, ethnocentric Anglo-Americans persistently impugned Mexicans' opinions, particularly when law and order were threatened. In the same way that the Texas Revolution and the Cortina War had cast doubt upon Tejanos' loyalty, so did three episodes in the postbellum period—the Cattle War, the Garza War, and the Spanish-American War.

The "Cattle War," which followed the Civil War and extended into the late 1870s, grew out of raids by Mexican nationals upon thousands of unbranded cattle which had multiplied for decades and now roamed the area between the Nueces River and the Rio Grande. Anglo-Texan ranchers, who had moved into the region in the 1850s and after, claimed the cattle as an extension of their own herds and engaged in a "war" with the rustlers in the region, and even in Mexico, where they went to retrieve their stock at times and also to deal with the raiders. Along with other white residents, the cattle ranchers immediately associated Mexican Americans in the region with the desperadoes. According to testimony given before a congressional committee in Washington, Tejanos of South Texas entertained a violent antipathy toward *gringos*[48] and in other ways retained their Mexicanness. As one witness put it, they were "Mexicans in feeling, thought, language, religion, and everything."[49] They were a floating population that voted on both sides of the border, noted another. Most lived in Mexico while working in the United States and all the while conspired with the cattle thieves, who quite likely were the Mexicans' kinfolk, "their cousins, uncles and brothers."[50]

Yet, evidence submitted to the same committee and testimony from other sources upheld the allegiance (and "Americanism") of Mexicanos. Military officers and residents of the border described them as excellent members of society and still others as "good, honorable, law-abiding men, citizens of this state and fully entitled to the protection of the law."[51] The committee bore testimony that the great majority of them were honest, industrious, and laborious people, who also suffered greatly at the hands of cattle thieves.[52] Governor Richard Coke described them in 1875 as excellent citizens, well disposed and loyal to the Texas government.[53] But in 1874, when reportedly confronted with the Mexican consul's complaint that Mexicanos were being deprived of their lives in Texas without the form of law, the same governor was rumored to have retorted: "If you do not want your people treated so, let them keep out of the country."[54]

During Catarino Garza's abortive attempt at revolution against Mexico's President Porfirio Díaz in the 1890s, Mexicanos in the border counties who sympathized with Garza also incurred attacks from Anglos who thought of them as an anarchistic lot without ability to distinguish between good and evil causes. For years, the well-educated, liberal, controversial, and Texas-raised Garza had been publishing journalistic denunciations of Díaz from his various newspaper headquarters in Eagle Pass, Corpus Christi, and Palito Blanco. Finally in the summer of 1891, Garza and his followers, many recruited in Texas, set out for Mexico from Starr County, determined to overthrow Díaz. Their strategy was thwarted by troops from Fort Ringgold, however. Retreating toward Duval County, Garza made it and the border region his base of operations. From there, Garza continued to agitate against Díaz and prepare other invasions of Mexico. United States authorities sought to suppress the movement in South Texas but encountered difficulty as many Tejanos assisted Garza to elude the law.

Expectedly, Anglos associated Mexican Americans in the area with what they considered Garza's quixotic and irresponsible cause. The *Galveston Weekly News* described Garza's ranks as lawless, ignorant, lower-class Mexicans easily led into undertakings promising adventure or gain, a small army comprised of individuals who were residents of both sides of the river with no ties to either country.[55] Captain John G. Bourke of the Third Cavalry, sharing his knowledge of the situation with the U.S. Secretaries of War and State, distinguished between two kinds of Mexicans. First, those who reside in towns such as Laredo, Brownsville, Corpus Christi, and San Diego were decent people who stayed away from involvement. But there was a second, more belligerent class, "made up of the worst elements that ever stood in the way of civilization." This constituency was Mexican in origin and speech, yet "very anti-Mexican and anti-American." They were utterly devoid of principle, they lived a hand-to-mouth life, and they were an extremely undesirable people. Bourke viewed them as generally sympathetic to lawlessness.[56]

In a white country where Mexicanos faced an almost perpetual demand that they prove their loyalty, it was to be expected that whites would manifest their doubts about Mexican allegiance in more extreme ways. Though this occurred numerous times throughout the century, the most fantastic display of overreaction took place as the United States participated in a "splendid little war" thousands of miles away. In late April 1898, as American forces engaged Spain in its last stand in the Western Hemisphere, reports circulated that *peninsulares* and *criollos* living in Mexico were going to conduct guerrilla warfare along the Texas border by paying volunteers for filibustering expeditions. According to ex–Ranger Captain J. S. McNeel, recently returned from Mexico, desperate characters were to raid Texas, destroy property, and commit crimes of different sorts.[57] Fears that Mexican nationals would aid in an attack on the United States with the tacit consent of the Mexican government produced suspicions that the Mexican American element in Texas was involved as well.[58] From Austin, apprehensions circulated that Mexicanos of DeWitt and adjoining counties were becoming warlike. According to allegations, they were organizing into armed bands that threatened to destroy American property and commit murder should whites resist. Colonel Fred House, a veteran from DeWitt County, reported that, when Mexicanos learned of the war with Spain, "they became insulting and arrogant toward Americans." They were, complained the indignant House, asserting defiantly that the state belonged to Mexico and that they were going to use the present opportunity to good advantage to get it back.[59]

In Victoria, whites quickly inquired into meetings Mexicans had been holding.[60] Citizens in DeWitt, Karnes, and Gonzales counties were much alarmed at the feared movement of Mexicanos. Reports circulated that strange Mexicans, allegedly coming from the Rio Grande border, were appearing in that area; that individuals were bragging and making threats of what they were going to do. Throughout the state, Anglo veterans offered to come out of retirement to raise volunteer companies to nip the feared un-American uprisings and halt the possible Mexican invasion. House himself called upon the governor for authority to raise a company to maintain order among the lawless element. In San Diego, some forty men joined a company of minute men and readied themselves for the call of danger. In Beeville, a local division of the Knights of Pythias prepared for work in the event of border troubles.[61]

Nothing materialized; the threats were groundless. Victoria learned that its Mexican citizens had no sympathy for monarchical Spain and were supporting the Cuban rebellion, their meetings possibly having a connection with the upcoming Cinco de Mayo celebrations.[62] In Beeville, where similar fantasies circulated, a local paper assured readers that Mexicanos were democratic in their politics and had no sympathy for Spain: "In this country the Mexicans have long ago expressed themselves on the Cuban question by the organization of a league for the purpose of contributing to the relief of the patriots of the island."[63] Not only that, but many Mexicanos in the border areas volunteered to join in the war against Spain.[64]

Actually, the Tejanos' lack of patriotism was more of a figment of the white mind than a reality. The many critical comments Anglos made on the issue throughout the nineteenth century were logical extensions of their view that Mexicanos who were racially and culturally different could not have patriotic feelings similar to their own. But this view also reflected the general conservative tenor of white society, as it perforce made Tejanos appear threatening whenever they took that conservatism to task. For despite Anglos' expectations of indolent Mexicans, Tejanos were readily attuned to things around them. It was the problem of Mexicans meddling where whites did not want them that engendered accusations of ingratitude and subversion.

6. Leyendas Negras

An astonishing number of Mexicans in the nineteenth century fell victim to lynch law and cold-blooded deaths at the hands of whites who regarded the killing of Mexicans as inconsequential. Indeed, the entire race was often the object of demands calling for their decimation by white men. Violence against colored peoples was nothing novel: it had, in fact, long been rationalized on the grounds that blacks were part of a state of "beastly living" and Indians were similarly part of a condition of "primitive savagery." Mexicans did not have the traits that whites characterized as "beastly" or "savage" in blacks and Indians. However, Anglos did see a kinship between Tejanos and red "savages" and black "beasts" and, more importantly, a difference from themselves. The 1821–1900 period was a time of intense frontier strife, and interaction among red, white, and black pressed upon whites to maintain their hegemony over darker-skinned peoples through any means. As had been the case since the seventeenth century, Americans also needed to see violence in others to conceal the depravity within themselves.

Given the image whites held of mixed-blood Mexicans and the state of frontier conditions, then, Tejanos were grouped alongside blacks and Indians in a category of animal-like people, and racial antipathy toward Mexicans frequently matched hatred of the other two groups. In all three cases, violence was inflicted without guilt.

No white man necessarily sat down to think long and hard in hopes of detecting some essence in Mexicans that qualified them for categorization as inhuman. Yet travelers and settlers coming into intimate contact with Tejanos in the Central and South Texas areas in the 1840s and 1850s did tend to think along these lines. One reason often given by whites for this attitude was that Mexicans had descended from ancestors who exhibited depraved and barbarous conduct.

A few found Spain's long reputation of producing stock inclined to perfidious, cruel, wanton, sadistic, and atrocious acts conveniently applicable. Interestingly, only in attributing brutal passions to them did whites concede to any degree that Mexicans were in fact Spanish; to give them Spanish attributes otherwise was to grant them an identity that could be equated with civilization and whiteness. That would negate all the other attributes upon which Anglo attitudes rested.

According to this point of view, the violent propensities in the Spanish character had been amassed during the centuries of racial *mestizaje* in the Iberian Peninsula, especially with the Romans, before Spaniards came to America and mixed with Indians. The Spaniard was therefore an atypical sort of man whose biological constitution thirsted for carnage. Teresa Vielé, an army officer's wife on the Texas border, relating what an indelible impression the Mexicans' kindness had made on her, still maintained that "mild and inoffensive as they usually are, they have enough Spanish blood left in their veins to be occasionally roused to deeds of desperation and bloodshed."[1] Editor John Salmon "Rip" Ford's disquisition on the inherent cruelty of Mexicanos, published in his *State Times* (Austin) was indicative of the white racial fancy that inherent depravity within Mexicans was a legacy of the Iberian character. Reporting on the bullfights held in mid-century San Antonio's San Pedro section, the editor ventured into an editorial to explain the depravity in white society's midst:

> *Señoritas* of Mexican lineage graced the occasion by their presence. Their dark eyes would flash with excitement when a fellow narrowly escaped a horning. The American flag was flying over the pen. God forbid it should ever be desecrated to a like purpose. There is something revolting to humanity in these exhibitions. When attended by all the pageantry of banners, and trumpets, and scarfs, and beautiful women and brave men in gorgeous costumes, it is but a piece of garish cruelty; divest it of those, in its own reality it appears a slaughter of brutes to gratify an unhallowed desire to witness scenes of barbarity and bloodshed. Bullfights are calculated to render the heart callous to the sufferings of others. They inure the eye and the mind to the sight of bloody deeds. They cause gentle woman to smother one of the most lovely and appreciative feelings of her heart, pity—and the universal benevolence of the sex, which impels them to bind up the wounds of the afflicted, and to

pour balm upon the bruised and crushed spirit. They accustom
all classes to the unmoved contemplation of death scenes;
slow, lingering and tortuous. Byron when writing on the sub-
ject as exhibited in Spain, spoke thus of its tendencies:
   "Such the ungentle sport that oft invites
   The Spanish maid, and cheers the Spanish swain
   Nurtured in blood betimes, his heart delights
   In vengeance, gloating on another's pain.
   What private feuds the troubled village strain,
   Though now one phalanx'd host should meet the foe
   Enough, alas! in humble homes remain
   To mediate 'gainst friends the secret blow
   For some slight cause of wrath, whence life's warm stream
   must flow."
Between bull fights and gladiatorial shows there is but one
step, prize fighting. All are founded on a disposition to pander
to the worst passions of our nature, and deserve the unmiti-
gated condemnations of every good citizen. The morbid and
depraved appetite which required exhibitions of wanton cruelty and refined modes of torturing animals and men out of
their lives should not be fed. The actors and the audience in
these dramas of criminal cruelty are both guilty, the first as
principals, the second as accessories. They end in degenerat-
ing, and inhumanizing the masses.
   Spain might have been a more powerful nation, had not her
bloody conquests, the character of her national sports sapped
the fountain of humanity of sympathy in the breasts of her
people. The butcheries practiced by her soldiery in America
were reflected by her bull fights and implanted a deadly social
poison in every age, sex and condition of her citizens. She
stood before the world a spectacle of blood. The crimson floods
from millions of human beings incarnadine the whole nation.
In her might she was full of ruthlessness and violence and
murder. In her decay she is destined to drink still deeper of the
bitter cup of retribution, and it may be that the chalice will be
held to her blood stained lips by the hands of her own children. Here is moralizing quite enough for bull fighting.[2]

   If whites could impute to Tejanos a cruel European heritage,
they could just as well establish that Mexicans were the offspring,
on their maternal side, of an Indian civilization itself particularly in-
famous for similar barbarities. Though this theme did not find full

expression in the 1821–1860 period, the Texans who expressed ideas about the inhumanity of Spanish civilization can hardly have been ignorant of Aztec practices of human sacrifice and ritual cannibalism. That brutality had been well known long before 1821. In 1858, the editors of the *Texas Almanac* did touch upon the idea that the mixture of Aztec with Spaniard led to depravity in two already defective civilizations. Jealousy was a potent element in the moral constitution of the Cis-Atlantic Spanish race, they wrote, "as it is with all men who wear the *virtues* loosely about them." This jealousy, continued the editors, had not been at all mitigated by the union with the Aztec aborigines of Mexico, but had rather increased among their hybrid descendants.[3]

Views of the barbaric Mexican, rooted in the conviction of depraved Spanish and Mexican-Indian civilizations and in the notion of aberrant miscegenation, probably achieved firsthand affirmation in the white mind with the war atrocities of the Texas Revolution.[4] After the events of 1836, this image held firm. Texans feared more invasions from Mexico and perhaps other Alamo and Goliad type massacres. These were not baseless apprehensions, since Mexico did send troops into the Republic in the early 1840s and Mexican agents were actively inciting the Indian tribes against the Texans. Anglos' cognizance of Aztec-descended or at least Indian-blooded Mexicans allying themselves with the red men of the prairie fearfully reminded them of the Mexicans' imputed ferocity. A number of other violent confrontations in Central and South Texas in the 1850s buttressed their fear of treacherous Mexicans.

According to those who commented on this theme, the Mexicans who coexisted in Texas society were indeed volatile and temperamental. They were cowards, an anonymous traveler asserted in 1837, but, like all others of their stripe, cruel to those about them, even tyrannical and bloodthirsty when their opponent had no power to resist. They would not retaliate when bested, he continued, but pride at that point gave way only to the desire for revenge, "which smolders like hidden fire until it can be gratified without the hazard of open, manly attack."[5] The large amount of crime in San Antonio, Olmsted thought, was the byproduct of Mexican avarice and revenge. These passionate motives were not rare, he was told.[6]

Once set in the notion that Mexicans had inhuman emotions, that they were not the equal of white people, that they were more like blacks and Indians, Anglos dispensed with Mexicanos as if they were no more than animals. Those were the attitudes expressed by a group of men in 1837 when a Mexican attempted to "break" a mule after they had failed. The life of a Mexican was of no value, they felt, and it made little difference whether he was killed trying to tame the animal or not.[7] The larger society shared the same sentiments. Olmsted found whites around Victoria regarding Mexicans "in a somewhat unchristian tone, not as heretics or heathens to be converted . . . but rather as vermin, to be exterminated."[8] It was as if society did not bar the killing of Mexicans.

Mrs. Peggy McCormick, on whose estate the major portion of the San Jacinto dead lay slain, was another Anglo who apparently considered Mexicans as less than human beings. Three days after the battle, the Mexican corpses still remained unburied, an intolerable stench permeating the air. Mrs. McCormick called at the headquarters of Sam Houston requesting that the "stinking Mexicans" be removed from her land. According to John J. Linn, a resident of the town of Victoria, the general replied to her in feigned seriousness, "Madam, your land will be famed in history as the classic spot upon which the glorious victory of San Jacinto was gained! Here was born, in the throes of revolution, and amid the strife of contending legions, the infant of Texas independence! Here the latest scourge of mankind, the arrogantly self-styled 'Napoleon of the West,' met his fate!" The landowner snapped back: "To the *devil* with your glorious history. Take off your stinking Mexicans."[9]

But Mrs. McCormick was not the only one lacking human decency. A Mexican colonel lamented: "More intolerable [than the treatment of myself and my fellow prisoners of war] was the stench arising from the corpses of the field of San Jacinto, which they (the Texans) did not have the generosity to bury, after the time-honored custom, regardless of their health and comfort, and those of the surrounding country."[10]

The image of Mexicans as semi-human objects may also explain how the lore developed about Mexican bodies remaining intact when unburied. For certainly it took a mind that had the most uncaring regard for Tejanos as people to argue that even animals did not scavenge on Mexican corpses as they did on those of animals or individuals of other races. But the belief had its backers. Thus did Noah Smithwick, who had been in Texas since the 1820s, explain that buzzards and coyotes feasting upon dead horses following the Battle of San Jacinto passed up the Mexican dead "presumably because of the peppery condition of the flesh." Moreover, continued Smithwick, when cattle nibbled at the bones that scavengers had known better than to touch, their milk was adversely affected.[11] Likewise officer Samuel French, after surveying the dead at the field of Palo Alto where one of the first battles of the Mexican War had been fought, maintained: "The flesh of the Americans was decayed and gone, or eaten by wolves and vultures; that of the Mexicans was dried and uncorrupted, which I attributed to the nature of their food, it being antiseptic."[12] And after eleven Mexicans were reported lynched along the Nueces River in 1855, a Corpus Christi correspondent declared it was just as well: "Better so than to be left on the ground for the howling lobos to tear in pieces, and then howl the more for the red peppers that burn their insides raw."[13]

If these pre–Civil War attitudes toward Mexicans reflected ideas growing out of attitudes toward miscegenation, the struggle of the Texas Revolution, and the contacts made by Texans imbued with Manifest Destiny, the postwar feelings were connected to more localized matters. In this period, whites were pushing into unsettled and hostile areas and trying to tame the southern and western frontiers. More and more contacts were being made with Mexicans, either because whites were pushing into areas of dense Hispanic concentration or because Mexican immigrants were entering the state in greater numbers. Since there was increased necessity to justify violence toward Mexicans, whites articulated the idea of Mexican brutality more forcefully during this era. That need explains why whites continued to believe in this brutality when long association with them was enough to show that Tejanos were no more savage than they themselves.

Thus, the two decades of Civil War and Reconstruction did not erase the old ideas about Mexicans descending from brutal ancestors. In connection with Cuba's war for independence from Spain (1868–1878), for example, the *San Antonio Express* published a discourse (taken from the *Washington Chronicle*) that argued that the history of the Spanish race was one of cruelty and blood. "Whence this temper of the jungle is derived, whether from a truculent and Moor-hating ancestry, an infusion of Saracenic blood, or that climatic influence which breeds the desert asp and arms the jealousy of the South with the stiletto of the assassin, we will not stop to inquire," it said.[14] Others, also searching for the origins of this bloodthirstiness on the paternal side, traced it to the Roman influence on the Iberian race. W. M. Walton, narrating the life of the outlaw Ben Thompson, commented on the kinship between the Italians and Mexicans. Though this was not a widely known fact, he cautioned, a remarkable likeness existed regarding lasting passion and devotion to revenge.[15] Among Mexicans, the vendetta is practiced as persistently as among Sicilians, declared the *San Antonio Express* in its coverage of Uvalde rancher Hewlett Griner's murder in a Mexican town across from Del Rio, Texas. "They are as constant in their hatred as their friendships."[16]

And concerning the Mexicans' origin on the maternal side, some question may be raised as to why Mexicans were referred to so frequently as "Aztecs."[17] Perhaps the "Aztec" label expressed for whites the depravity they wished to see in Mexicans. After all, had not Aztecs, like Spaniards, lusted for carnage, practicing torture, human sacrifice, and cannibalism?

If Texans had associated Tejanos with bloodshed in the antebellum period when the contact with violent Mexicans had been less intensive, the racial clashes of the 1870s and after brought the "savage" Mexicans almost to the gates of the citadel of white hegemony. This was the time which most demanded the reduction of Mexicans to the status of violent and depraved humanity, for the test to white supremacy called for Anglos to muster all their powers to quell Mexicanos in the battlegrounds of South and West Texas. The state government itself felt the challenge, and often it was from Central Texas cities like Austin and San Antonio that police forces were dispatched to assist white residents in the beleaguered regions. Hence, during this period Anglos scrutinized the Mexican temperament more meticulously, attributing violent impulses to every facet of the Mexican nature—cultural forms, family relations, their treatment of animals, their view of death, and other aspects.

Thus, whites pointed to cultural traditions that testified to the depravity they attributed to Mexicans. Cockfighting, wrote a correspondent for the *Beeville Bee*, may seem very cruel to an American, "but with the Mexican it is a great thing."[18] In San Antonio, an observer signing himself "Stranger" noted that at the cockpit in the Mexican quarter, Mexicanos found both horror and pure joy exhilarating. "The excitement is upon the part of horror, and is improper, while the moral effect cannot but be attended with evil results," he concluded. "The law in most states is very strict upon this game, and it is to be hoped that it will not be long tolerated in Texas."[19]

In many parts of the state Anglos depicted Tejanos in the same light—as depraved and brutal men with a violent disposition. The editors of the *Brownsville Ranchero* in November 1867, for example, accused the local Mexican element of being inclined to cruelty and sadism. Not that it suggested that the people of Brownsville were uncivilized, qualified the paper, but half of them were less than half-civilized, and the rest did not show much enlightenment by tolerating cruel and barbarous acts. "Beyond any sort of doubt there are stronger evidences of barbarism on this border than exist anywhere else in the United States, and the American element has allowed itself to be dragged down to witnessing what would not be tolerated in any civilized country," reproached the paper, claiming that cruel treatment of animals and even small children was common. "But worse than all is the murderous spirit among the aborigines of this border. Murder, robbery and stealing have to be entered as concomitants of the general brutalizing and barbarous practices before spoken of." The paper called for laws for the protection of animals, children, and other recipients of alleged Mexican mistreatment.[20]

Furthermore, it was said that Mexicanos showed no concern about killing another person, made no scruple about taking another life; their character was so impervious to emotion that they wholly disregarded the value of human life. Though some whites may have come to this conclusion from their personal acquaintance with Mexicans, the numerous reports printed in newspapers (and reprinted throughout the state) about Mexicans knifing one another and killing their countrymen in seemingly savage ways further solidified Anglo fantasies of the Mexican as an especially insensitive, degenerate creature.

Such stories circulated in disproportionate numbers as compared to counterparts involving whites. In fact, Anglos regaled themselves by reporting those of a more hideous kind. In June 1897, for example, the *San Antonio Express* devoted conspicuous coverage to what it called the "most heinous crime known in the annals of Wilson County." In Floresville, it wrote, Máximo Martínez killed a man and a woman, then "outraged" and murdered eighteen-year-old Juanita Acosta in "the greatest crime ever committed in Texas."[21] In October of that year, the same paper reported an equally gruesome deed, "the ugliest crime ever committed in Duval County," that of two Mexicans accused of terribly maiming a child in Hebbronville.[22] The *Beeville Weekly Picayune* in 1899 reported a similar case of child abuse, describing it as the most "blood-curdling cruelty and inhuman barbarity ever brought to light in Bee County." The paper said that justice required that both the adults' necks be broken "and without any more delay than is absolutely necessary to allow the law to take its course."[23]

Editors often did not take the trouble to check the veracity of their correspondents' communiqués—after all, they confirmed what Anglos were already predisposed to believe. Again, it was the *San Antonio Express* which reported in 1891 the diabolical murder of a Mexican woman in Del Rio. Allegedly, in the absence of her husband, she had allowed a visiting Mexican man to share her household overnight (which reaffirmed something else whites had been saying about Mexicans). The man, after satisfying his lust, knocked her in the head, then literally cut her to pieces with a sharp hatchet. Having accomplished this butchery, the *Express* continued, "he wrote on the wall in Mexican language 'Fresh Meat for Sale' in letters of blood and then skipped out presumably crossing the river."[24] An even more horrible tale had come to the *Express* from the *Denver Tribune*, via the *Cincinnati Times Star*, in 1880. Antonio Mestes, after knocking his wife down with a club, seized a knife and with it savagely lacerated the lower portion of her body, cutting out immense pieces of flesh. Mestes then deliberately ripped open the womb, took the still living child she was carrying, and, throwing it upon the floor, stamped the life from the infant. "After this he tore the body of his wife almost apart, and after further mutilations fled." Mestes himself met death at the hands of a lynching party.[25]

Cases of Anglo murders at the hands of Mexicans received extensive coverage in the press, magnifying the image of the Mexican who harbored a taste for human blood. When the *Victoria Advocate* reported Martín Rodríguez' murder of Deputy Sheriff Thomas A. Shaw in 1877, it meticulously described the wounds the Mexican had inflicted upon Shaw: a deep, long gash in the left shoulder, a small one above it, two small holes in the right side—in front and back—where a long slender knife had been driven clear through the body, two cuts in the hand, and a blow on top of the head.[26] In the same way the *San Antonio Express* described the story of the murder of merchant A. Grossard in Laredo by a Mexican in 1879. Grossard's head had been battered and mutilated by repeated blows from a hatchet, the bloody instrument having been left upon the throat of the victim. The brain protruded from one horribly gaping wound, one of the eyes had been disengaged from its socket, and the face was disfigured beyond the semblance of human recognition.[27] The *Austin Statesman* was equally graphic in reporting the 1885 axe murder of Thomas Merrill and his wife at their ranch in El Paso by Mexicans. Mr. Merrill's head had been cut and gashed, his legs mangled, and his face beaten in, related the article. Mrs. Merrill's neck was almost severed from her body, and her spine from the neck to the waist had been severed in two or three places. The culprits had lashed her head, broken her skull, and cut through her breast and into the heart.[28]

According to Anglo speculations, Mexicans relished the thought of death and murder in a way exclusive to their race. Those were the thoughts of the Eagle Pass correspondent for the *San Antonio Express* who reported the killing of a Mexican by compatriots in Eagle Pass in 1885. The large number of Mexicans who viewed the remains of the murdered man had brought to his mind the "noticeable fact" that whenever a corpse had been horribly mangled or had died a violent death, the Mexicans of the lower order flocked in crowds to view the repulsive sight. "They seemed to be possessed of a morbid curiosity in this line," he elaborated, "which psychologists can probably explain."[29]

Others further maintained that Mexicans were a people without appreciation for the lives of others. Jonathan Gilmer Speed, the *Harper's Weekly* correspondent, informed an avid public that Mexicanos living along the Rio Grande held life very cheap and "did not count it a grievous crime to murder either in private quarrel or public brawl."[30]

If Mexicans were evil and wicked in their rational state, when aroused they could commit acts of uncontrollable desperation, a number of students of the Mexican temper maintained. In its normal state, one citizen advised, the Mexican race was docile and tractable. Left alone, Mexicanos were indolent, listless, and lethargic, and, when commingled with the energy and vitality of Anglo Saxons, they became a gentle, useful and pleasant element of the social and political fabric. But once provoked by a sense of wrong, he cautioned, the Mexican race was vicious and implacable.[31] Indeed, a cowboy recalled, Mexicans were all right normally. "But when they got drunk they'd fight over almost anything—horses, saddles and gear, money or *señoritas*. They were quick on the draw and had red hot tempers."[32] Susan G. Miller, recalling her years in the Nueces Valley, agreed that an aroused Mexican sought carnage. Often, she noted, a certain *señorita* at a dance might stir a little jealousy: "And if some *señor* felt a keen pang of jealousy sweep over his soul that he could not resist, he immediately drew his knife and a murder or terrible slashing would result."[33] In a similar vein, Lee Harby assured his readers that, as far as riots and quarrels were concerned, Mexicans were law abiding. "But make no Mexican your enemy," he cautioned, "or else avoid the darkness of night and of shadow, should he be within reach. He will smile in your face as you pass, then wheel and sheathe his long, sharp knife in your back."[34]

If Mexicans were so treacherous, so base, so cruel, so inhuman in behavior, could they not be regarded (and dispensed with) in the same way as "beastlike" blacks and "savage" reds? Those were the feelings of numerous Anglos in the postbellum period, especially in the frontier areas where the greatest friction existed between the two peoples. During the Cattle War of the 1870s, even as they committed foul murders on Mexicans throughout the state, Anglos expressed threats of extermination "upon all of the race they can meet with."[35] When the *Corpus Christi Weekly Caller* received a report that crime was rampant among Mexicans in Rio Grande City, it opined that what Starr County needed was a few first-class executions to teach a certain class of people "to have more respect for human life"![36] In the opinion of an army officer serving on the Texas frontier, the only possible way to catch the followers of Catarino Garza and suppress the uprising he led was to employ several regiments of cavalry and have a great roundup of "greasers" in the neighborhood in which Garza and his men were known to be, "and not to be too nice about killing a lot of them."[37] Following a feud in Presidio County, white cowboys contemplated the extermination of Mexican sheepherders in the summer of 1897.[38]

Whites dehumanized Mexicans to such an extent that some considered them no better than animals. Robert Maudslay, a West Texas sheep rancher, related matter-of-factly that dead men in those parts disturbed practically no one in the 1890s, "especially if the dead man was a Mexican." When on a certain occasion a dead Mexican was found in the middle of the road, whites simply drove or rode around him, unconcerned about the body. "It was nobody's business to bury him."[39] In Junction, Mary Jaques related the story of a Mexican threatened with lynching in the early 1890s for suspicion of rape. What the Mexican's fate was she never knew, but had he been a Texan, she thought, it would probably have fared very differently with him from the first. "But it is difficult to convince these people that a Mexican is a human being. He seems to be the Texan's natural enemy; he is treated like a dog, or, perhaps, not so well."[40]

Predictably, the pre–Civil War condescension which held that even scavengers could distinguish between the bodies of Mexicans and others continued in the 1870s and 1880s. In 1884 a person identifying himself as AMIGO notified the *Corpus Christi Weekly Caller* that a Mexican suspected of having stolen a horse had been recently killed by the horse owners just west of Corpus Christi. "They buried the dead Mexican on the spot without a coffin. Some might ask, cannot San Patricio afford a coffin? *Que diferencia?* If what is told be true, that coyotes refuse *chili* seasoned Mexican *carne*, he will rest in his grave as quietly as if deposited in the tomb of Capuleto."[41] Marshall T. White of Carrizo, elaborating on the vileness of "greasers" to the *Philadelphia Sun* in 1886, pronounced Mexicanos involved in the border troubles in that time "cursed rank clear through—soul, body, and bones." In the war with Mexico, he continued, the bodies of American soldiers and the carcasses of "greasers" were often buried near each other. Wolves would dig up Americans' bodies and avoid the corpses of Mexicans sticking halfway out of the ground beside them. The beasts apparently knew enough not to eat Mexicans because "Greasers fill themselves with cayenne pepper and garlic until their flesh is as rank as mule meat."[42]

In short, the image whites held of Mexicans as depraved and brutal folk determined the careless regard Anglos held for them as human beings. Whites seldom manifested guilt or restraint in committing acts for the preservation of white supremacy. Indeed, the same violent repression whites exhibited in East and Central Texas against blacks throughout the nineteenth century, the same rigorous methods they used in West Texas to remove the Indians from the path of settlement, found their counterparts in South and West Texas in relation to Mexicanos. Whites dealt with blacks, Indians, and Mexicans as if they were animals of the field. But there was an imbedded peril in carrying out such violence, for Tejanos were not entirely defenseless. What if, in those areas where they predominated, Mexicans did to whites what whites were doing to Mexicans?

7. Frontier "Democracy" and Tejanos—the Antebellum Period

The image of the cruel, vindictive, blood-lusting Mexican troubled many a Texas white in the nineteenth century. But, whereas the black threat to white supremacy inevitably assumed a sexual cast in the white mind, whites manifested little fear of sexual revenge from Mexicans. Stories of white women raped by Mexican men were rare. What whites feared in Mexicans was the potentially violent depravity they imputed to them—something readily identifiable, considering the violent temper of the era. Patterns of hysteria emanating from Mexican threats were followed inevitably by hasty and vicious white retaliation. The reprisals, the lynchings, the wanton murders not only evidenced the white desire to teach Mexicans about keeping to their station, but also attested to the violent nature of the nineteenth-century white citizen in the Lone Star State.[1]

However much whites contrasted Mexicans with themselves, they could hardly have imagined them so radically different as to erase the probability that Mexicans harbored parallel attitudes about the dispensability of Anglos. The tensions and anxieties produced by the necessity to keep a colored people subordinate quite naturally fostered fears that Mexicans sheltered ambitions and desires to employ violence like that which whites used to preserve order. Not surprisingly, whites constantly expressed suspicions and anticipations of possible vengefulness. Conscious of how impossible it would be for *any* person not to be vengeful under the circumstances they imposed on Tejanos and, far more importantly, how vengeful they themselves would be in similar conditions, whites lived in dread of falling victim to the cruelty they ascribed to Mexicans.

No wonder that a police body like the Texas Rangers emerged amid this violent setting. From a small body of volunteers charged with scouting against Indians in the 1820s, it became a corps that enjoyed the tacit sanction of the white community to do to Mexicans in the name of the law what others did extra-legally. Frightened whites came to depend upon violent men to suppress the cruel streak so much feared in Mexicans. Visitors and citizens alike could hardly fail to notice the quality of men making up the force. Mexican War Officer John Pollard Gaines, on passing a company of Rangers, described them as "an ugly looking set of customers" whom he fancied as possibly more troublesome to the citizenry than the Indians whose depredations they were responsible for suppressing.[2] Samuel E. Chamberlain, on his way to Mexico to participate in the Mexican War, described the rangers he met at a drinking and gambling saloon as a "reckless, devil-may-care looking set [which] would be impossible to find this side of the Infernal Regions. With their uncouth costumes, bearded faces, lean and brawny forms, fierce wild eyes and swaggering manners," he went on, the Rangers typified the outlaws of the state.[3] Another military man, Albert J. Myer, depicted them similarly in the mid-1850s. "Do not picture the Ranger as you read of him in newspapers, as brave and reckless but with a redeeming trait of chivalry," he explained to his prospective brother-in-law in New York:

> The Rangers are rowdies, rowdies in dress, manner and feeling. Take one of the lowest Canal drivers, dress him in ragged clothes—those he ordinarily wears, as you see him, are altogether too clean—put a rifle in his hand, a revolver and big bowie knife at his belt—utterly eradicate any little traces of civilization or refinement that may have by chance been acquired, then turn him loose, a lazy ruffianly scoundrel in a country where little is known of, less cared for, the laws of God or man and you have the material for a Texas Mounted Ranger, an animal—perhaps I should say a brute—of whose class some hundreds are at present mustered into the service to fight Indians. There are exceptions. My invective is not meant for all.[4]

The Rangers' persecution of Mexicanos remains largely an undocumented story, partly because Ranger records are not easily accessible to researchers. Most historians still adhere to the interpretation presented by Walter Prescott Webb, who depicts the Rangers as "quiet, deliberate, gentle" men committed to upholding law and order and taming the Texas wilderness for decent folks.[5] But the portrayal by observers who saw them in their times and the tales that have come down through the years within the Tejano community go some way in verifying the reputation of *los rinches* as range riders who tyrannized Mexican Americans with the acquiescence of white society.

In this early period, they thrived because the memories of the massacres of the Alamo and Goliad were still fresh in people's minds. In Central Texas, where Anglos pushed into Tejano population pockets in the years immediately following the revolution to consolidate their gains, recrimination against the natives followed swiftly and haunted them until the time of the Mexican War, when other causes became the impetus for their harassment. Though suspicion of disloyalty and the wish to dispossess Mexicans of their land played a part in this, the desire for vengeance against depraved humanity was certainly a motivating factor.

Obviously, harsh treatment of the defeated enemy follows most if not all wars, but in the case of the Tejanos of Central Texas, the only ones with whom white society had much contact up to the late 1840s, the degree of retaliation seems surprising. Mexicanos in this area were so few in number that they posed practically no threat to white supremacy. They were not in possession of any great wealth of land that was absolutely essential for whites to have. As a group, they either had remained neutral during the revolution or had sided with the Texans. But, influenced by their image of Mexicanos as a colored people and a part of the wilderness in the way of civilization and by their belief that they had revealed themselves as a vicious people without human sensibility during the war and that similar perils still lingered, Texans responded with an enmity which evidenced their opinion of Tejanos as nonpersons.

Retaliation against Tejanos came swiftly in the form of forceful banishment by Anglos who saw nothing wrong in displacing a people with generational ties to their homes and regions. It appeared also in the form of violent depredations by lawless men who assumed the right to harassment just because Tejanos were Mexicans. In Victoria, the Mexican families who had founded the town just twelve years earlier were expelled from their homes immediately after the Battle of San Jacinto by incoming Anglos who accused the residents of disloyalty.[6] In 1839, white outlaws still circulated around the neighboring country preying upon remaining Tejano *rancheros*, who found themselves helpless to recover their stolen stock.[7] In the early 1840s, the Victoria city council ordained that the mayor could apprehend any persons suspected of spying for the Mexican government and jail them for further investigation. Mexicans entering the city were required to report to the mayor and obtain a pass within twelve hours after arriving; and they were not to leave without notice. The council also authorized the mayor to examine persons without visible means of livelihood and remove such persons from the town limits.[8]

The Tejano population of Goliad encountered a similar fate in the aftermath of the revolution. The Texas army robbed and plundered homes, driving the local population out.[9] In 1839, those in the ranching areas near the town lived in constant dread of being murdered by the same bandits who were stealing cattle from the Tejanos around Victoria. During the summer, these bandits gave warning of their intention to visit Carlos' Rancho (where residents from Victoria and Goliad had taken refuge in 1836) in order to burn it down and kill all the Mexicans belonging to it.[10] The threat did not materialize until three years later, when Anglos angered over an invasion from Mexico destroyed the ranch and compelled the families to leave the Republic.[11]

In Nacogdoches, Tejano families were continuously robbed of their livestock, grain, and belongings after the revolution. In 1838, trouble intensified between the Mexicans and Anglos, and in the ensuing conflict, many Mexicans were killed or expelled.[12]

For a while, at least, San Antonio escaped these troubles, mainly because it was further removed from Anglo settlements. But as whites drifted into the area in the late 1830s, it became "an open field for their criminal designs," according to Juan N. Seguín, mayor of the city in 1841–1842. At every hour of the day, Seguín wrote, Bexareños came to him seeking protection against harassment by white adventurers. "Could I leave them defenseless, exposed to the assaults of foreigners, who on the pretext that they were Mexicans, treated them worse than brutes?" he asked.[13]

The threat of vindictive Mexicans perpetrating the same sort of violence on white society that Anglos had inflicted on Mexicans came first not from Tejanos but from Mexicans from Mexico. Twice in 1842, military forces sent by Santa Anna invaded the Republic. As would be the case in other "mass" threats to white supremacy, Anglos responded swiftly. In the first case, Tennesseans, who had come to the rescue of Texans before in 1836, left for the Republic posthaste. Organized as the "Wolf Hunters," a volunteer group founded explicitly to avenge the capture of San Antonio in March 1842 by General Rafael Vásquez, they swore to protect Texas from the Mexicans, those "imbecile, oppressive, priest-ridden pusillanimous and semi-barbarous" people. These "Wolf Hunters," upon arriving in Texas to hunt for the Mexican "wolves," found the Mexican "savages" practically nonexistent, the punitive venture turning into a complete fiasco.[14]

The later invasion led by Adrian Woll (a French soldier of fortune employed by Mexico) more prominently raised the specter of a Mexican challenge to white supremacy and produced the predictable intemperate acts against Tejanos who were implicated. Woll entered San Antonio on September 11, 1842, and seized the town, but after ten days, he began his evacuation to the Rio Grande. Upon reaching the Medina River, he found more than 150 carts belonging to Mexican citizens of Béxar, "loaded with furniture and the little that was left to those wretched people by Texan rapacity." The families were making their way to the villages on the Mexican side of the Rio Grande, fearful that the Texan volunteers would return to San Antonio and take revenge upon them. A couple of days later, four Tejanos caught up with Woll, having escaped after being "inhumanly treated by the barbarians."[15] Those who remained in San Antonio did in fact experience the wrath of irate Anglo volunteers. According to one of the participants, the soldiers acted "very badly, having ventured to force the Mexican families from their homes, to droop about in the woods & seek shelter wherever they could find it. Moreover in order to gratify their beastly lusts compelled the women and Girls to yield to their hellish desires, which their victims did under fear of punishment & death." Members of the Alexander Somervell expedition, who were to retaliate against Mexico for the Woll attack on Béxar, averred plainly that it was their intention to capture and kill the last surviving Mexican on the continent.[16]

Within a few years, however, Anglos no longer felt the threat of Mexican invasions. After Texas' annexation by the United States in 1845 and the Mexican War of 1846–1848, resentment against Tejanos for their participation in the Texas Revolution and their complicity in the Mexican invasions was less evident. But violent attacks against Tejanos did not cease, for friction based on numerous issues, including xenophobia and the problems of the 1850s, persisted. Further, Anglos were pushing into South Texas and brushing against a new Tejano population zone. Impudence or challenges to the authority of white persons incurred quick and decisive retaliation.

Thus, Zachary Taylor's soldiers, at Corpus Christi with the Army of Occupation from July 1845 to March 1846, lost no time in retaliating for the killing of one of their members by Mexicans at a local dance. The whites "headed a party and made an informal call upon the revelers, killing four men, burning every *jacal* on the bluff, and running every Mexican off the hill into the brush."[17] Likewise, white citizens in 1863 took rapid action upon hearing that two white men had been killed near a camp of Mexican cartmen. According to the *Goliad Messenger*, Anglos went to "clean up" the site.[18]

Lynching, as a form of retaliatory violence, also surfaced during the antebellum period, though not with the same fervor and vindictiveness as after the Civil War. When the first Tejano fell victim to extra-legal execution is unknown, but by the 1850s lynch law was being applied in the Central Texas areas. Olmsted reported that in San Antonio, whites had shown no scruple about lynching a Mexican who attempted to steal a horse, hanging the man on the spot where he was apprehended.[19] And near the Escondido Creek, a Mexican who killed a cow in August 1857 was summarily lynched.[20]

The hanging of Chepita [or Chipita] Rodríguez in San Patricio in 1863, while a legal execution, might just as well have been a lynching. It was the product of vindictive emotions desiring recompense for the murder of a white man. To protect its stability, white society was willing to go to the extent of executing an innocent woman.

As the story is known, Chepita Rodríguez and her father arrived in the San Patricio area in 1836, fleeing Santa Anna's recent rise to power in Mexico. Within weeks, her father was dead, killed in a local skirmish with Colonel José Urrea's troops, then making their way toward Goliad as part of Santa Anna's efforts to suppress the Texas rebels. Alone in Texas, the young woman took up with a passing cowboy and soon bore a son. The relationship ended abruptly when the cowboy deserted her, taking the infant with him.

Then, in August 1863, two men arrived at Rodríguez' cabin on the banks of the Aransas River. One of them, the story maintains, looked very much like the cowboy she had known years before. Surely, this was the little boy who had been stolen from her by the drifter. The next morning the young man was gone, along with the money belonging to his partner, who now lay dead, killed with Rodríguez' ax. Seeking to protect her supposed son, Chepita Rodríguez wrapped the deceased's body in burlap and with the assistance of Juan Silvera, a retarded individual who lived nearby, carried the body to the river. A few days later, however, the body washed ashore and suspicion fell upon Rodríguez and Silvera, the only people who lived upriver. The sheriff arrested them forthwith.

Cattlemen along the Aransas River area quickly raised talk of lynching them, reasoning that the lack of a jail might lead to their escape. Only with the protection of the sheriff's father, who happened to be the state representative from the district, were Chepita and Juan able to elude the vigilantes, who soon appeared at the representative's home demanding that he release them from his custody.

When she was tried in October 1863, the jury found Chepita Rodríguez guilty, though it recommended her to the mercy of the court on account of her advanced age and the circumstantial evidence. The recommendation, however, did not move the judge, for he ordered her hanged, while sentencing Silvera to five years in the penitentiary.

Her execution was carried out despite doubts over her guilt. The sheriff never identified the man she was accused of killing and did not prove a motive other than robbery. According to the stories that persisted long afterward, the sheriff arrested her on account of pressure that he solve the murder. The judge similarly submitted to demands that he do something about avenging the death of an Anglo.[21]

The case serves as an example of how extreme Anglos were in their persecution of Tejanos suspected of offenses against whites, for Rodríguez' execution was exceptional in the way the law dealt with women in the American West. During the entire nineteenth century, very few women were hanged, and most of those had committed extraordinary crimes. In California, only one woman was lynched—a Mexicana by the name of Juanita who allegedly killed a white man in a mining town in 1851 for making improper sexual advances toward her.[22]

If Texans would go to the point of executing Chepita Rodríguez, a harmless woman who posed practically no threat, it is not surprising that they reacted ruthlessly when faced with group efforts against them. From the 1850s until the end of the century, Anglos experienced a number of assaults from Mexicans seeking to amend perceived wrongs. Whenever this happened, the episode invariably took on the coloring of a disorder grander than its scale—and whites responded punitively. When, as mentioned above, a Mexican horse thief met death by lynching in San Antonio, his friends threatened retaliation. The sheriff, under the pretext of subduing another "riot," called for an armed posse of 500 men, hoping to get rid of a large part of the neighboring Mexican population in the process. This plan failed when others did not join as anticipated.[23] Another "riot" occurred on New Year's night, 1854, involving Mexicans and white teamsters and soldiers at a *fandango* in Corpus Christi. Pursuing the retreating troops toward their quarters, the Mexicans stabbed two of them, one fatally. Incensed at what they considered the cold-blooded murder of their comrade, the whites set their minds on revenge.

About twenty-five of them subsequently went into the *fandango* grounds and set fire to four *jacales*. An innocent Mexican who happened to ride up at that time was killed by gunfire from the whites. A heavy military guard was posted in the city to prevent further difficulties.[24]

In 1857, a "Cart War" erupted between whites and Mexican cartmen who monopolized, through lower charges, the hauling of food and merchandise between San Antonio and the coast.[25] The antagonism probably grew out of the movements against Tejanos since 1853, encouraged by the bitter political divisions that had emphasized race and religion. As early as April 1855, accounts had circulated that the Committee of Vigilance assigned to keep Mexicans out of Guadalupe County had destroyed Mexican carts in the Seguin area.[26] Then, late in the summer of 1857, Anglo freighters, bent on erasing this "subversion" of free enterprise, began the harassment and assassination of Mexican cartmen, the waylaying and destruction of carts, and the pillaging and confiscation of valuable cargoes in the area between San Antonio and the coast. According to a member of the state legislature, these outrages may well have represented a movement to deprive Mexicanos of the privileges and immunities guaranteed by the Treaty of Guadalupe Hidalgo.[27] The affair attained such emotional heights that some feared a race war, others a "campaign of death" against Mexicanos.[28]

However indifferent whites had been to the treatment of Mexicans earlier, these hostilities were so obviously vindictive that at least a segment of the population rallied to the cartmen's defense, although there was some indication that their motives were economic rather than humanitarian. A few called for an immediate end to the "war," fearing the demise of economic prosperity; others complained about the rise in prices as Mexicans no longer dared take the old routes; still others called for patrols to protect their commerce.[29] The *Southern Intelligencer* opposed the attacks because "No generous mind could palliate this war upon a weak race, laboring as we all do for bread. If we permit the driving out of the Mexican laborers, a war upon the Germans will come next—and that in turn must be followed by a war between the poor and the rich."[30]

Others of course did show humanitarian sentiments. San Antonio appointed a committee of citizens to investigate the difficulties leading to the attacks upon the inoffensive cartmen.[31] The *Nueces Valley Weekly* argued likewise, albeit unable to extricate itself from the prejudices of the day:

There is evidently a large amount of prejudice existing among our people against the greaser population, which often breaks out in acts of violence and lawlessness, altogether indefensible. The fact of their being low in the scale of intelligence is no excuse for our making them the scape goats for all the outrages that have been committed during the progress of this unfortunate war. Let us rather, by better examples and kind treatment, endeavor to elevate their moral and social condition, thereby making them respectable members of our community.[32]

Eventually the affair was suppressed through a combination of pressures from the Mexican Minister in Washington, Manuel Robles y Pezuela, and U.S. Secretary of State Lewis Cass, acts of the legislature, military escorts for cartmen, and volunteer companies organized to bring about order, often through lynch law.[33] Karnes County, however, was unrepentant as late as December 1857, when citizens meeting there criticized the reaction of the governor and the volunteer companies. While denouncing the conduct of citizens who had taken the lives of Mexicanos, they nevertheless regarded the "continuance of Peon Mexican teamsters on this road as an intolerable nuisance, and request the citizens of San Antonio to withdraw them and substitute others, or procure some means to prevent them from committing depredations upon our property at times when it is impossible for us to guard and watch over it."[34] In Goliad County, where a local paper had threatened in the summer of 1857 that "the first offense committed by *armed Mexicans* in this *section* will be the signal to sweep them from the face of the earth," similar resolutions were passed.[35]

The episode that sent the most chilling tremors of fear into the world of white Texans during the antebellum era, however, was the Cortina War (discussed above in Chapter 5), which coincided with the anxiety that settled portentously over the entire South following John Brown's October 1859 raid on Harper's Ferry. On October 8, 1859, an official in Austin dramatically sent news to President James Buchanan of an outrage on the frontier at Brownsville, its character "so flagrant and astonishing that I would not believe it possible, if the information were not on undoubted authority."[36] An investigating committee in the 1870s described the affair as having no parallel in history. A single *ranchero*, defying the law, had captured a sizable town with a band of friends, laid siege to it for five months, defeated the forces of the state, and kept the Mexican flag flying over his camp, then retreated to Mexico to resume the fight.[37]

Cortina's movement escalated into a "war" because of the setting and the emotional circumstances surrounding the threat that
he posed to white supremacy. For one thing, whites were very much
alert to their minority status on the frontier, where Mexicans outnumbered them ten to one; in certain communities along the border
the proportion was twenty-five to one.[38] This awareness surfaced repeatedly in their pleas for aid. Stephen Powers, using his influence as
Chief Justice of Cameron County and Mayor of Brownsville, informed the President that some ninety poorly armed white adults
were residing in a county populated largely by Mexicans.[39] A special
to the *New Orleans Picayune* similarly emphasized that the twelve
thousand people in the area were much nearer to Brownsville than
the people in the suburbs of Gretna and Algiers were to New Orleans, and of those, "no more than over 300 men, women, or children sympathize with Americans."[40]

Second, a guilt complex magnified the Anglos' worst fears:
whites knew well that it was they who had alienated the native population and provoked the antagonism of the threatening Mexicans.
Thus the paranoid fear that Cortina and his party were out to hang
every white in the area.[41] According to special correspondent "G" of
the *Corpus Christi Ranchero*, Brownsville had learned from reliable
sources that it was the intention of Cortina's band of "greaser *pelados* to exterminate the *gringos* on the river."[42] Further fears circulated that throughout the entire border area the hearts of peon
masses were "throbbing and pulsating in perfect unison" with the
revolutionists, the rumors fanning fears that others of their kind
would swarm across the Rio Grande.[43] What commenced as a riot, a
San Antonio paper remarked, had developed into an insurrection,
and then a war; what had begun as a foray of banditti was now a contest of races, perhaps heading for a war of nations.[44]

Whites hundreds of miles away mirrored the local hysteria. In
Nueces County, settlers felt especially vulnerable to Cortina's ca-
pricious advances. Reports circulated that Mexicans from both sides
of the Rio Grande were advancing toward the area, intent on exter-
minating every white inhabitant and reconquering the country as far
as the Colorado River.[45] At Goliad, a citizens' committee issued the
alarm that Cortina's robbers were killing whites when apprehended,
and that an excited Mexican rabble in the streets of Brownsville was
crying for death to Anglos. The committee reported Cortina moving
toward the Nueces at the head of an estimated 1,500 men with the
avowed intention of murdering and breaking up the white settlements, and, to make matters more terrifying, "exciting insurrection
among the slaves."[46]

The defensive posture whites assumed in these interior areas illustrated the dreadful seriousness with which Anglos took Cortina's challenge. Nueces County residents appealed to whites in Victoria, Goliad, Refugio, Karnes, and Live Oak counties to come with arms and ammunition to rescue them in "this deserted and unprotected frontier."[47] They also formed a military company of about one hundred men, the Walker Mounted Rifles, to protect all portions of the country and adjacent ones in the emergency.[48] Citizens of Banquete in Nueces County meantime put together a committee to appoint scouts to range the countryside between the town and the scenes of Cortina's depredations and to give timely notice of his movements. They resolved further to form themselves into a minute company, to act in unison with the committee of safety in Corpus Christi.[49]

The theme of Mexican cruelty was reiterated in tales of butcheries and other gruesome incidents, confirming white suspicions that Mexicans were in search of gore. Cortina was reportedly mutilating the bodies of those unfortunate enough to fall his victims. Whites visualized a foe of "atrocious savages, who would as soon beat out the brains of an infant as shoot an undoubted spy."[50] The "greasers" were sparing no one, neither child nor woman.[51] In late January 1860, when the rebellion had been all but suppressed, some still displayed profound anxieties over the "deep-seated hostility in the breast of every Mexican against all *gringos*," including children.[52]

Much of this was in the mind: in the end more Mexicans than whites perished. Numerous observers affirmed that the Cortina scare was exaggerated beyond its actual proportions. General David Twiggs, commander of the Eighth Military Department in San Antonio, and others wired the Secretary of War that, in their estimation, reports of the Cortina "War" were greatly amplified.[53] But to those close to the crisis, the threat was not at all imaginary. The people of Brownsville called for "protection with a vengeance."[54] As a local paper put it, the "rebellion must be crushed out and disposed of forever, and Cortina and each and all of his adherent outlaws tracked, caught, and exterminated, and this by the most prompt, energetic and efficient measures."[55] Indeed, several years after the troubles, suspected participants were still being hanged.[56]

When white men slaughtered hundreds of Mexicans while shouting "Remember the Alamo!" and "Remember Goliad!" at the Battle of San Jacinto, they prefigured the kind of violent relationship which was to exist between whites and Mexicans in the Lone Star State. For after that victory, there was no need for further violence against Mexicans, no chance that Mexicans would ever again reign over whites in Texas. But through violence, Anglos expressed their blatant dislike for Mexicans—a loathing founded on a congeries of undesirable qualities imputed to them in the areas of race, culture, morality, and patriotism. Through such deeds whites expressed their conception of "greasers" as being akin to blacks and Indians, their distaste for the Mexicans' looks and racial characteristics, their contempt for Tejano "cultural backwardness" and resistance to learning Anglo ways, and their acute awareness of differences between themselves and Tejanos in language, religion, and even eating habits. And such actions as lynching Mexicans accused of crimes, committing atrocities during riots or wars, and attempting in various ways to repress Mexicano citizens before they began thinking that they were "just like white men" was to reach an even greater magnitude in the years following the Civil War.

8. Frontier "Democracy" and Tejanos—the Postbellum Period

After 1865, whites sounded repeated alarms manifesting old fears. Even more than before, they conjured up visions of Mexicans doing to them what they were doing to Mexicans and imagined terrors that evolved into exaggerated fantasies far more frightening than the actual threat. Any assault on the white racial order, any disturbance involving Mexicans was classified under the rubric of "uprisings," "insurgencies," and "riots"—in a context of possible massacres. Treacherous, violent Mexicans were considered capable of nothing less.

In part, this was a reflection of the era, the most violent in Texas history. During this time, Central Texas was embroiled in a wide variety of violent episodes growing out of troubles from the Civil War and Reconstruction, outlaw activity, vigilantism, community feuds, agrarian radicalism, and political agitation. Simultaneously, Anglos throughout the state faced the most severe resistance from colored peoples—by riotous and uppity blacks in the old plantation region, by intransigent Indians making their last stand in the western frontier, and by unneighborly Mexicans.[1] It was in this era that the colored thread of multiracial society posed the greatest challenge to the white racial order.

This was the period in which Anglos were seeking the redemption of South and West Texas, when they were encountering Mexicans in a crusade to rescue the wilderness from backwardness, indolence, and disorder. Along the Rio Grande and in an area extending to the perimeters of Central Texas, white supremacists and the feared blood-lusting Mexicans clashed. In this charged atmosphere, where Anglos were out to vanquish that which they should not become, the underdog very naturally assumed an image of a fiendish and vindictive foe.

In turn, those fears brought out the most vicious instincts in

Anglos themselves, for only violence checked the lingering dread that Mexicanos might seek vengeance and recompense in some insane rage. Moreover, violence served to vent the ingrained contempt Anglos had for "greasers." The Texas Rangers were abolished during the Radical Reconstruction period, but they were reorganized in 1874 and in the following years they enjoyed an even more lenient license than before to dispose of Mexicans threatening the white citizenry of southern and western Texas. Their ranks continued to consist, as a South Texas resident testified in 1878 before the Committee of Military Affairs in Washington, of a class called "cowboys" who as a group were wild and reckless and resisted all discipline.[2] In the 1870s and 1880s, the Rangers carried out a campaign of terrorizing the Mexicans of the Rio Grande Valley (and Mexico) at every opportunity on the premise that the more fear they created, the easier would be their work of subduing the Mexican raiders. Their tactics included harassing residents of Brownsville and breaking up *fandangos* there.[3] When artist Frederic Remington visited "Big Foot" Wallace in the latter part of the century, he found it hard to believe that other Rangers he knew and respected could be in a class with Wallace, an old Ranger who had come to Texas to kill "greasers" because his brother and cousin had been killed in the Goliad Massacre (he felt by the end of his days that he had avenged their deaths). "For the tale of their prowess in Texas always ends, 'and that don't count Mexicans, either,'" noted Remington. "The bandit never laid down his gun but with his life; so the '*la ley de huga* [*fuga*]' was in force in the chaparral, and the good people of Texas were satisfied with a very short account of a Ranger's fights."[4]

The Rangers thrived because of the terrifying image whites conjured up of cruel Mexicans. Fears were evidenced in hysteria, overreaction, and retributive violence. With all of white society ready to strike against any Indian or black threat with a harsh, brutal, often extralegal form of violence, it is small wonder that the everyday citizen, the vigilante, and the Texas Ranger joined in retaliation against Mexicans as well.

Wherever Anglos found the need to correct some transgression committed by Mexicans upon white society, they acted with dispatch and resolution. In Central Texas, where Mexicans were by no means immune from the fury concentrated to the south and west, a party of white avengers in 1868 indiscriminately executed seven Mexicans near Boerne on suspicion of murder;[5] and in Goliad County, a mob lynched Juan Moya and his two sons in 1874 for allegedly killing an Anglo family.[6] Further south, around the Nueces

County town of Banquete in the mid-seventies, a band of whites killed some forty Mexicans "just as they came upon them on the ranches, roads and wherever they were found" in retaliation for the killing of a man named Rabb, a local rancher described as a desperado and a murderer (he was alleged to have killed a Mexican), the terror of his neighbors and often his friends.[7] In the West Texas mining town of Shafter (Presidio County), Anglos in 1890 crushed local troubles with assistance from the state. Uneasy feelings arising from the lynchings of a Mexican by Anglos had been growing for some time. Ultimately, things culminated in a confrontation between the two races when peace officers visited a Mexican dance one Sunday night to establish order. Forced to retreat to the center of town, the officers waited for Texas Rangers and workers from neighboring mines to assist them. Upon being reinforced, they quickly re-entered the Mexican quarter and muffled the resistance. The governor subsequently assigned a large force of Rangers to guard the surrounding country.[8]

Continued disturbances which Anglos found menacing naturally led to fabrication of stories and distortion of reliable reports. In April 1886 a *San Antonio Express* correspondent, assured that his sources were of good authority, reported a party of Mexicans taking over Collins Station, located forty miles west of Corpus Christi. According to his story, Deputy Sheriff P. S. Coy, whom the bandits suspected of murdering one Andrés Martínez, notified the businessmen of Collins that he had information of a possible attack and that the raiders planned to kill him in order to collect the $1,000 reward posted by the deceased man's father. Fearing the burning of the town, the informant continued, the male population shouldered their guns and readied for an attack. Despite these preparations, a large crowd of armed Mexicans succeeded in capturing the town and, posting sentinels, searched every house for Coy without apparent success. In the end, the reports proved baseless. When the expected crisis passed, both Anglo and Mexican citizens of Collins declared the accounts vile fabrications and false in every particular; the town had not been invaded, nor was Coy anywhere in the vicinity. Two Mexicans suspected of being the murderers of Martínez were at about the same time found hung at Los Indios Ranch, near Benavides in Duval County.[9] The San Antonio *Freie Presse* two weeks later circulated reports that it had been Corpus Christi, not Collins, that had been attacked, a charge vehemently denied by the *Corpus Christi Weekly Caller.*[10]

A similar sort of fantasy found its way into the *San Antonio Ex-*

press of June 30, 1896. The paper alluded to an organized band of Mexicans heading toward the city to "slaughter the gringo." According to a letter received by the city marshal, the streets of San Antonio would soon be flooded with gore and the population of the Alamo City would be reduced perceptibly. The report noted that the Mexicans had not set the date for the "gringo hunting expedition," but, when carried out, its goal was conquest or death. The feared attackers stated the following grievances:

> Being protected by the law, the "gringos" and the Germans rob the laborer of his hire all over Texas and when they don't resort to murdering the men, they drive them off their ranches and run them out of the country. There is something wrong with the country. You ought to regulate the scales of justice of the statue on top of your court house. Then the Italians, the negro, and unfortunate Mexican, the Spanish, the French, the Cuban, and not the Germans and the "gringos" alone would receive fair treatment, and then, too, the statue would represent Justice, not Infamy.[11]

The threat apparently never materialized, for the local papers published no further news of it.

Given the almost constant presence of such rumors and the fear that they could develop into veritable bloodbaths, whites found lynching to be an effective way of meeting these perils and teaching Mexicans to mind their place. The amazing number of lynchings, it is true, were not necessarily restricted to blacks and Mexicans, for they were characteristic of violent Texas. But lynchings of blacks and Mexicans were accompanied by ritualistic tortures and sadism not displayed in other lynchings—such treatment being justified by reference to the supposed sexual threat posed by the blacks and the cruelty and depravity of the Mexicans.

Lynching and other forms of extralegal retribution, which had surfaced as whites made greater contact with Mexicans in the pre–Civil War era, ran rampant in the late 1860s and the 1870s, primarily in the focal areas of South and West Texas, and did not abate in the remaining two decades of the century. Such deeds often expressed irrationality and personal vindictiveness. In Brownsville the murder of a Justice of the Peace led to the swift lynching of the Mexican culprit, all whites present participating in the hanging. Then "while hanging but just before his pulse had ceased to beat, a stranger with flowing cape and slouched hat, embraced the body and lifting his own feet from the ground so as to throw greater weight on the murderer, muttered, 'That's the way we used to do them in Californy.'"[12] Jesse Sumpter, a white on friendly terms with Eagle Pass' Mexican American community, related the gory incident of a Mexican lynched for killing a white boy and absconding to Mexico with a fourteen-year-old white girl. When apprehended, the Mexican was turned over to the girl's father for surrender to authorities at Uvalde. But a lynching party took the prisoner behind the hills half a mile from town, gathered wood, and began building a fire. With the fire lighted, the party commenced torturing their victim. According to Sumpter, who showed reluctance to participate in the lynching, the whites mutilated the Mexican's nose and ears and split his hands and feet with their knives. The party severed various members of his body, gouged out his eyes, and finally picked him up and threw him into the fire. The Mexican, still alive, tried to scramble out of the fire, only to be flung back into the flames. There he was kept until life was extinguished. Mexicans of the area watched the ordeal from a distance.[13]

In Cotulla, a similar display of white wrath occurred in 1895. When Mexicans allegedly rustled a calf from rancher U. T. Sauls, the cattleman, along with Deputy Sheriff N. A. Swink, followed in hot pursuit, overtaking the suspected Mexicans at a roadside camp a short distance north of Twohig. Subduing them, Sauls attempted to search the wagon for the yearling. In the exchange of fire that followed, Florentino Suaste shot Sauls, while a Mexican man and woman received injuries and a six-year-old Mexican boy was killed. Excitement and strong talk of compensation immediately crystallized around the Pearsall and Cotulla areas, the inflammatory excitement exacerbated by reports of the recent killing of Tom Hughes at Kenedy by another Mexican. After a preliminary hearing, Suaste and two Mexican women were charged with murder and remanded to jail without bail to await the action of the grand jury. Later, some eight or ten masked men entered the county jail, overpowered the jailer, took his jail keys, and carried Suaste down near the Nueces River, there swinging him up to a mesquite limb and riddling his body with bullets. In the ensuing inquest, a local judge rendered the verdict that Suaste had come to his death by hanging and gunshot wounds inflicted by unknown persons.[14]

In January 1896, Aureliano Castellón met an atrocious death for paying romantic attentions to a white woman. Trouble grew when Castellón began making advances to fifteen-year-old Emma Stanfield, sister of Hugh and Watson Stanfield. The Stanfields, indignant over the Mexican's persistence, warned him to make no more visits to the girl's home. But Castellón continued in this forbidden venture. His mutilated body was found perforated with eight bullet holes and burned almost beyond recognition on the roadside near Senior some time after these admonitions.[15]

Considering the many incidents that either purported to be or proved so threatening, it is not surprising that the "riot" came to rival any other sort of threat during this era. Some of these so-called riots grew out of personal confrontations between individual Mexican and Anglo men; others resulted from Mexicans amassing in protest of some deed perpetrated against their people; still others occurred when Mexicans collectively sought to remedy the injustice of the racial order. There were few incidents during these assumed riots in which Mexicans actually attempted to do the sort of things whites feared. Exaggeration nevertheless became a characteristic outgrowth of these confrontations. Vindictive retaliation, so much a concomitant of the apprehension that Mexicans could or might reign over whites, inevitably ensued.

In mid-April 1886, an encounter between Mexicans and whites at Alpine led to reports that a riot had erupted. According to newspapers, racial tensions had been mounting and culminated when Mexicans raided a local saloon, killing a number of white patrons. When news of the raid spread, armed whites living in the town and neighboring areas cleared it and the surrounding country of Mexicans, killing a number of the Mexican residents in retribution.[16] In September of that same year, two Mexicans, assisted by two whites, killed a couple of officers and a civilian and injured half a dozen others during an election in Karnes County. The county attorney dealt with the "riot" by immediately wiring the governor for assistance, calling upon the Texas Rangers to capture the escaped Mexicans and their cohorts.[17]

But there were also, in the latter part of the nineteenth century, riots of a much greater magnitude that seemed to embody the white nightmare of Mexicans exercising unrestrained depravity. The Laredo riot of April 1886, an interracial riot in which seven-eighths of the participants were Mexicans, generated a concern out of proportion to the affair, perhaps because "depraved Mexicans" were on the loose in a white man's land. The heat of a political campaign between the two local political parties, the Guaraches (Sandals) and the Botas (Boots), threw Laredo into what one newspaper described as a "Blood Lust."

The riot grew out of the defeat of the Guarache party and the decision by the Botas to celebrate their victory with a mock funeral of the deceased Guaraches. On April 7, the day after the election, at a bit past 5:30 P.M., the Botas, some 150 strong and armed because of threats from the Guaraches, started their procession through downtown Laredo. Suddenly someone discharged a weapon, and there followed a general exchange of fire between the two forces, which seemed to be equal in numbers and comprised of both Mexicans and Anglos (though the Mexicans far outnumbered the Anglo marchers in both parties). Property was destroyed and at least eleven people were killed (both whites and Tejanos) and many others injured. Soon after the battle, however, local troops from Fort McIntosh appeared and restored peace.

In the meantime, telegrams from the military at Fort McIntosh, private citizens, and law authorities had been sent to Austin. Responding to the frantic wires, the governor declared martial law, ordered out the state militia, and dispatched a company of Rangers to the scene. But by the time the special train with the militia arrived from San Antonio, Laredo was pacified. The militia remained in charge of the town for the next two days, the Rangers staying for some time thereafter.[18]

More ominous than any other was the Rio Grande City riot of September 1888. It epitomized, for a very short time, the inverse order so much feared of the depraved, brutal Mexican supreme in a world turned upside down. Its origins went back to May 1888, when the sheriff of Starr County, W. W. Sheley, charged Abraham Recéndez with robbery. Recéndez was then killed by Sheley's companion, Victor Sebree, who alleged that Recéndez was "trying to escape." General consternation among Mexicanos and a deep feeling of resentment against whites, and principally Sebree and Sheley, occurred, especially as Sheley had been previously implicated in the lynching of several Mexicanos. In Corpus Christi, Catarino Garza, who was then agitating against Porfirian rule through his newspaper *El Comercio Mexicano*, wrote editorials charging Sebree, who was U.S. Inspector of Customs, of "foully assassinating" Recéndez. In Rio Grande City, the affair found its way into city politics when Augustine and Silurio de la Pima [Peña?] organized a political faction to oppose Sheley and began to use the murders as examples of racial prejudice. The Pimas, according to reports at the height of the riot, had incited "Mexicans against Americans" and had encouraged a "race war." Garza had moved to Rio Grande City in the meantime and became involved in the affair when employed by the Pimas to be part of the editorial campaign against the political opposition. Soon, Garza encountered

Sebree, and in a melee that followed on September 21, Sebree shot Garza.[19]

Sympathizers of Garza threatened to lynch Sebree and followed him out of town as he fled to refuge in nearby Fort Ringgold, where the post commander ordered the two-hundred-man mob to disperse. Mass hysteria followed. Alarming telegrams reporting fear and bloody war raging on the Texas frontier poured into the governor's office in Austin. Messages from Starr County reported rampant anarchy on the border and called for troops, as lives of white citizens in that region were said to be in imminent peril. Other dispatches told of uncontrolled rioting, of armed men parading the streets in control of the city and county, of telegraph wires cut, of officers of the law being intimidated, of newspaper correspondents prohibited under penalty of death from sending information on the true state of affairs, of over one hundred Mexicans trying to lynch Sebree, of fears that a general massacre of white citizens was certain unless the three companies of United States troops from Fort Ringgold came to the rescue.

Amid all this, whites were very cognizant that Rio Grande City, like Brownsville in 1859, was an isolated community, nearly one hundred miles from Laredo and the nearest railroad station. They were equally aware that the Rio Grande was a broad, shallow river in that particular area, making it easy for Mexicans living in Camargo and other towns in Mexico to cross over. More ominous, Mexicanos outnumbered American settlers ten to one, which, according to one newspaper, made them arrogant and aggressive.

Whites called upon all the help they could summon. They wired the Secretary of the Treasury, pleading for Washington to order the military at Fort Ringgold to protect the custom house and citizens until all danger had passed. In the meantime, part of the Third Cavalry was ordered to reinforce Fort Ringgold. But this was not enough. Pleas went out to the governor to send the entire Texas Ranger force (the *Beeville Bee* hoped that the Rangers would slay some of the rioters). The governor telegraphed the sheriffs of Cameron, Hidalgo, and Zapata counties to proceed by forced march to the troubled district. He also wired the San Antonio and Belknap Rifles and the Houston Light Guard to prepare to march on a moment's notice. The border sheriffs eventually commanded 150 followers, in addition to 100 volunteers gathered by the Béxar sheriff. The riot eventually petered out by itself, although the presence of troops from Fort Ringgold contributed inevitably toward its demise.[20]

In August 1894, a race riot involving Mexicans broke out in

Beeville. While not threatening the white racial order, it neverthe-less achieved significance, considering the elements involved— Mexicans versus blacks. According to reports, tensions between the two groups had been mounting as a result of the gradual Latinizing of the county labor force. Beginning in the early 1890s, Mexicans from the western counties had begun migrating into the Beeville area, competing for jobs with the local unskilled labor element, comprised mostly of blacks. White employers had contributed to the friction by hiring Mexicans at less than the usual pay to blacks, while throwing the latter into the unemployment pool; in fact, even whites complained of being unable to get decent wages for their la-bor. The discontent culminated in a raid upon the Mexican quarter. Blacks, accompanied by some "wild white boys" (according to the *Beeville Bee*), "Ku-Kluxed" the Mexicans, rocked the *jacales*, and intimidated the "Aztecs," telling them to leave the country lest se-rious punishment be inflicted upon them. Mexicans were badly treated wherever they resisted, one being cut over the eye with a brickbat, another sustaining a fractured arm from a club, and yet an-other appearing in court the next day with clotted blood in his ears. Not surprisingly, the riot loomed more significant because blacks participated. Whites sympathized instinctively with the Mexicans. The *Bee* reviewed the consensus of the white denizens, noting that they considered the Mexicans more useful citizens, better laborers, more tractable and reliable. Compared to the blacks, continued the paper, Mexicans were quieter and more peaceable, less addicted to rowdyism, were not as shiftless, and, considering their frugal living habits, could work for less. The sympathy of the majority of the citi-zens seemed to be in favor of the Mexicans, reaffirmed the *Bee*.[21]

Laredo experienced another riot in March 1899, quite unlike the one thirteen years earlier. The city at the time was under smallpox quarantine measures adopted by the State Health Officer requiring that all exposed persons move to a house of detention. Problems be-gan as certain Mexicans showed reluctance to relocate members of their families to what was referred to as the "pest house." A "buck-shot argument" followed when law officers endeavored to disperse an assembly of Mexicans supporting two brothers who demanded that officers allow their sister to be examined for illness before her removal. Resisting, the crowd began throwing rocks at the officers, an unidentified member firing at the city marshal. The officers drew their six-shooters and a fusillade ensued. Mexican townspeo-ple attracted to the scene added to the wild excitement, taunting the officers with cries of "Down with authorities," and "Bring out your

Negro soldiers," an allusion to the Tenth Cavalry stationed at Fort McIntosh. As businessmen and prominent citizens became aware of the "riot," they descended from all directions, armed with shotguns, offering their services to the authorities in the enforcement of order. The next day, Captain J. H. Rogers, of Company E, Texas Rangers, went into the Mexican section searching for rioters and arms allegedly stored there for the next confrontation. Violence flared up again when the inmates of the house resisted, Rogers sustaining injuries. The remaining Rangers repaired to the scene of the action hurriedly, determined to avenge the death of one of their companions. In the meantime, local officials urged the governor to send the militia or United States troops, lest a similar occurrence take place. Washington followed up by ordering the militia forces at Fort McIntosh to assist local officials. The Rangers, however, successfully suppressed the "riot," aided by a Gatling gun and the presence of United States regulars who made camp in the center of the city to prevent further disruptions. Among the casualties were Agapito Herrera, who, having shot one of the Rangers, was immediately cut down by another Ranger; Margarito Herrera, who sustained injuries in the left shoulder and a broken wrist from Ranger buckshot; and another Mexican killed by being brained with the butt of a rifle.[22]

These numerous episodes did not restrict themselves to the urban scene, for contests for supremacy extended to the untamed rural areas. In the 1870s and early 1880s, a genuine era of lawlessness reigned in the Nueces Strip and what contemporaries called the "bloody peninsula"—the lower part of Presidio County lying along the Rio Grande for a distance of sixty miles.[23] Mexican nationals and a motley array of white ranchers, cattle rustlers, and cowboys repeatedly fought over unbranded mavericks on the frontier cattle range. There, in that racial battleground, Mexicans and whites gathered together, many of them of a desperate character and refugees from the law.[24] Killing an adversary was considered no crime. Law-abiding Tejano citizens were assassinated, and, on the other hand, policemen, travelers, and other Anglos were similarly waylaid and ruthlessly murdered.[25]

The conflict took on overtones of a contest for racial supremacy. Whites continued conjuring up fears of the depraved nature of Mexicans. According to a lady named Kate writing to another woman in Austin in 1874:

> This country [Lamar, Aransas County] is in a dreadful state of excitement at present. The Mexicans brutally murdered a man

and his wife last week, about twenty miles from here, and the whole country is in arms about it. There have been several Mexicans hung and some shot since then, and there is great excitement existing both among the white people and the Mexicans. There is trouble ahead, I am afraid, as the Mexicans clear to the Rio Grande swear vengeance against the whites. The white men are afraid, to leave their families for a minute, for fear they will be murdered. Several families came to Lamar yesterday for protection, and I don't know but what we all have to leave here, though at present this is thought to be a safe place, as there are no Mexicans here and none nearer than fifteen miles.[26]

Though Mexican nationals were the principal antagonists, Anglos implicated the entire native Mexican population as accomplices in the attacks. Throughout the ordeal, there was an intense awareness of numbers: up and down the Rio Grande, as well as around San Antonio, the population consisted almost entirely of Mexican laborers, ranchers, and shepherds,[27] and the great mass of inhabitants between the Nueces and the Rio Grande was composed of people of Mexican origin, their proportion to all other classes about nine to one, white inhabitants not exceeding three thousand in number.[28]

Tales and rumors circulated that the invaders were on a rampage promiscuously killing whites, capturing children and carrying them off to Mexico as slaves, and even violating white women. Cries, appeals, and pleas for amends grew plentiful. J. Ulrich, United States Consul in Monterrey, Mexico, advised Washington that only "the hard hand of force" would do in coping with the Mexicans, no halfway measures sufficing. One patriotic white begged his fellows to throw off their lethargy, take retaliation into their own hands, "and let the despoilers again hear the war cry which arose above the din of battle at San Jacinto and Bexar."[29]

Anglos dealt with the threats as if Mexicans were indeed in a class with black "beasts" and Indian "savages." Citizens and newspaper editors agitated candidly for lynch law, and vigilance committees operated freely with their endorsement. In other cases, ranchers used the opportunity to vent their wrath on innocent laborers.[30] In 1877, J. L. Hall of the State Troopers informed Adjutant General William Steele: "There seems to be a regular organization among some of the cattle owners for the purpose of killing shepherds that they may by this means rid that section of sheep raisers. Most of the Mexicans killed are of this inoffensive class."[31]

There is no telling how many Mexicans fell victim to the reprisals. *La Revista Universal* of Mexico City reported in 1869 on the Mexicans' predicament in a white country. The Mexicans of Texas, it noted, for years the victims of the hate and antipathy of race, were daily persecuted, outraged, and murdered. Texas Mexicans, according to the Mexican paper, had as of late incurred the wrath of "Rip" Ford and of Richard King, owner of the gigantic King Ranch. Its sources, the *Revista* claimed, revealed that both men had organized companies of rangers for the purpose of satisfying "their hunger and thirst of justice for the frequent crimes of cattle stealing committed on the frontier, attributed maliciously to Mexicans." Moreover, the paper believed, these self-styled vigilante bands had burned several ranches and killed many Mexicans of both sexes, without "any formula other than that accustomed by the Apaches."[32] A *New York Times* correspondent, assigned to seek full particulars on the condition of affairs on the Rio Grande border, discovered that in the latter part of 1877 more than a dozen whites had been killed by raiders and over one hundred Mexicans hanged or shot to death by their persecutors.[33]

The darkest hour of these border troubles occurred in March 1875, when Mexicans "raided" Corpus Christi. It came at the time when the cattle rustling situation had reached its greatest intensity and when certain other alarming happenings in Nueces County imperiled the security of white citizens. Tragedies seemed to be befalling whites in the area with unusual regularity. In January 1872, a Mexican laborer at the Eliff Ranch in the Banquete area entered the Eliff household looking for money. The Eliffs at the time were absent, as Mr. Eliff was away on business and his wife was out visiting a Mrs. Hunter, who accompanied her back to her house, where they unexpectedly found themselves confronted by the trespasser, with "ax in hand, a diabolical scowl upon his face, and his entire appearance was such that it impressed deeply upon the minds of those ladies, that he was maturing some terrible plot of desperation." Taking refuge in Mrs. Hunter's home, the women found themselves facing the Mexican once more, this time in the middle of the night. Breaking through the window, the robber alighted upon the covering of Mrs. Hunter, his motive being murder and robbery. "He laid his ax heavily upon her breast and commanded her to be silent, swearing that if she spoke a word that he would split the heart out of her." At this point, the seventy-two-year-old Mrs. Hunter reportedly mustered prodigious strength and wrenched the ax from her attacker and was able to ward him off. The Mexican was reported hung by a mob, although citizens of Banquete stated that he had met his death due to a loss of blood stemming from the breaking of the window, and that he had already perished when they came upon him.[34]

Then in August of that same year, the *Nueces Valley Weekly* reported "the most brutal outrage and atrocious murder ever committed in western Texas." According to the report, "fiends in human shape" had entered the home of William Murdock twelve miles from Corpus, their motive apparently being robbery. The Mexicans, before departing, tied the old man and left him helplessly lying on his face. The "devils incarnate" then set fire to the house, and Murdock was literally roasted alive.[35]

At about the same period, Alberto Garza, known as "Caballo Blanco" (White Horse), was active in skinning enterprises in the Duval County area, his ventures coming under the wary watch of Nueces County citizens. In 1873 Garza robbed and pillaged a store at Concepción in Duval County, then repeated his deed closer to Nueces County in late 1874, robbing a trading post at Los Olmos. There, Garza threatened the store owner: "Los de Tejas para mí no valen nada y me hace muy poco esto."[36]

Finally, in March 1875, a division of Mexican bandits raided Corpus. Whites retaliated with a vengeance; one of the bandits, after being held prisoner for four days, met his death at the hands of a lynch mob.[37] Vigilante committees took to the countryside and brutally outraged and murdered peaceable Mexican farmers and ranchers. Some of them thought the occasion fitting for evening out old scores with the Mexican residents in Nueces and neighboring counties.[38] Unable to get to the bandits responsible for the attack, whites concentrated their fury upon the poor Mexicanos living in the county.[39] Bands of whites then headed toward La Parra in Encinal County searching out Mexican squatters alleged to have stolen hides buried or concealed on their premises. The attackers burned down the *jacales* and killed a number of residents.[40]

Faraway El Paso, although immune from confrontations over cattle, nevertheless began experiencing friction of a racial nature by the 1870s. Tension had gradually been building up since the previous decade, when whites began monopolizing the nearby Guadalupe Salt Lakes upon which Mexican livelihood depended. The political feuding of the contesting white factions plotting for control of the lakes produced an emotional sort of violence with vindictive overtones. In early October 1877, the Salt War began.[41] Following the closing of the Salt Lakes to Mexicans and the subsequent killing of Don Louis Cardis, a Mexican sympathizer, Mexicanos exercised unchallenged supremacy until the end of the year. Whites suddenly found themselves embroiled in a situation where they were radically outnumbered. El Paso in that frontier age was a remote community without military protection, since earlier that year the troops stationed at Fort Bliss had been removed to Fort Davis. El Paso had a population of about 800; Ysleta, the county seat, had approximately 1,600; Socorro, four miles below the county seat, about 700; and San Elizario, six miles below Socorro, 2,000. Almost all of these citizens were Mexicanos; only eighty Anglos lived in the entire county. Moreover, the great number of Mexican nationals living across the river augmented the Tejano population. It was common knowledge that the Rio Grande was fordable for eight months in the year and could be crossed at many points without difficulty, and that inhabitants of the Mexican towns of El Paso del Norte, Saragosa, Guadalupe, and San Ignacio could easily cross into Texas, where many were related to Tejanos by family, business, customs, tastes, and religion. Together, Mexicans and Tejanos posed a formidable threat to the eighty Anglos.

It did not take whites long to grasp the racial implications of their predicament, that recompense for the stealing of the lakes could well end in murder. Anglos expected nothing less than unbridled passion, as the messages for outside assistance revealed. Sheriff Charles Kerber emphasized the "treacherous character of the Mexicans" in his calls for relief. The rebels, wrote a number of citizens (including some Mexicans of the ruling elite), were an ignorant, prejudiced, and bloodthirsty Mexican mob. To whites the atrocities and butcheries committed during the crisis must have emphasized what they thought the Mexican character was capable of if unrestrained. The Mexicans cut one Anglo's throat, stabbed him twice in the heart, then took his scalp, eyebrows, and beard. When Charles H. Howard, the killer of Cardis, met execution by a firing squad, Mexican members of the mob hacked and chopped at the body. The corpses of two other Anglos similarly executed were stripped and mutilated. The final report of the investigating committee concluded that one of the causes for the riot had been that the Mexicans, "after the fashion of an ignorant and hot-blooded race," had sought vengeance for the death of Cardis.

In response to pleas for aid, the governor ordered Texas Rangers to the area in late October. The U.S. Secretary of War answered calls from the governor (after the affair had subsided) by ordering troops to the troubled spot. Sheriff Kerber organized a posse composed of thirty men from Silver City, New Mexico. These volunteers, because "the exigencies of the occasion [did] not permit that delay which a wise discrimination in the choice of material would cause," included an adventurous and lawless element which began indiscriminate outrages on Mexicanos. The Rangers riddled two Mexican prisoners with bullets "unnecessarily and unjustifiably," slaughtered a Tejano and wounded his wife on the pretext that the Mexican had shot at them from inside his home, and committed or attempted rapes. The investigators in early 1878 recommended the establishment of a permanent post somewhere in the area to prevent a recurrence of the "war."

Among the last border episodes of a magnitude sufficient to trigger retaliation was the Catarino Garza "revolution" of 1892, discussed in Chapter 5. Thwarted in his attempt to invade Mexico, Garza made Duval County and the border region his base of operation. The native Mexican American element naturally became implicated in Garza's exploits, especially since he was a Tejano. In dealing with the Garza "war," whites harassed and persecuted Garza's followers or suspected followers. The army arrested Alejandro Gonzales, Garza's father-in-law, and brought him to San Antonio from his ranch at Palito Blanco. In affidavits, Gonzales swore that the military had stationed pickets or guards around the ranch, then arrested him without charges. Gonzales further alleged that Commander John G. Bourke had slapped him in the face, cursed him, and abused him in other ways until restrained by his subordinate officers.[42] Others swore that troopers had invaded Tejano homes and arrested Mexican Americans for no reason.[43] In late 1892, after the episode had subsided, violence persisted against suspected Garzistas.[44]

The usual anxieties accompanied the Garza movement. In August 1892, as rumors still circulated that Garzistas were concentrating in the Laredo section at La Gata (Encinal County), where Garza had organized his last band of revolutionaries in December the year before, it was ascertained that it would not take "Mexico, the United States, and the State of Texas" to disperse the suspects from regrouping after all. The gathering turned out to be forty or fifty vaqueros sent out by large stock raisers in Webb and Encinal counties to round up scattered stock.[45] Similarly, rumors circulated a few weeks later that one hundred Garzistas were regrouping in Zapata County. As it turned out, they were peaceful laborers attending a *fiesta* commemorating the Mexican national day of independence on September 16.[46]

The nemesis of ethnic prejudice in violent form continued for the remainder of the decade. It found its way inevitably into the White Cap movement of Central Texas in the late 1890s. In Hays County, White Cappers mailed notices to planters warning them not to rent to Mexicans and blacks (and to whites "at one-third and one-fourth only"). The vigilantes threatened those disregarding their notice with violence. In neighboring Wilson, Gonzales, and DeWitt counties, White Cappers similarly demanded that landlords discharge their Mexican hired hands and run off Mexican renters or suffer the consequences. But farmers in those counties were reported ready to protect Mexicanos.[47]

Clearly, fear of Mexicans and what they might do, should they find the opportunity to repay in kind what was being done to them, translated into conflict throughout the nineteenth century, especially in the postbellum period. Violence was thus both a result and a contributing cause of ethnic hatred and disdain for Mexicanos. In the uninhibited ambience of nineteenth-century Texas, where the society at large condoned such terrorism, frontier "democracy" was carried out with impunity and vengeance.

9. Epilogue: "Not the White Man's Equal"

Collectively, the many attitudes whites held toward Mexicans went hand in hand with attempts toward oppression. They buttressed the idea that Americans were of superior stock and Tejanos were not, rationalized an elevated place for whites and a subservient one for Mexicans, and justified the notion that Mexican work should be for the good of white society. Those attitudes were at the base of the world that Tejanos had to grapple with in efforts to live a normal life and were among the forces defining what roles those coming from Mexico should assume.

Judging from the few studies that touch upon relations between Anglos and Tejanos in more recent times, these entrenched ethnocentric and racist attitudes held their own for decades into the twentieth century. Segregation, blatant discrimination, disparaging names, and public abuse all reflected a state of mind redolent of the nineteenth century. So did the widely held belief that Tejanos were to keep a place subservient to their benefactors. In South Texas in the 1920s, according to one study of ethnic relations there, prescriptions of social etiquette clearly delineated an inferior role for Tejanos, who were expected to follow certain rules, the most obvious including

a deferential body posture and respectful voice tone. One also used the best polite forms of speech one could muster in English or Spanish. One laughed with Anglos but never at them. One never showed extreme anger or aggression towards an Anglo in public. Of course, the reverse of this was that Anglos could be informal with Mexicanos; they could use "*tú*" forms, "*compadre*" or "*amigo*" and shout "hey, *cabrón*" or "hey, *chingado*" (son of a bitch) in a joking, derogatory way. Anglos could slap Mexicanos on the back, joke with them at their expense, curse them out, in short, do all the things people usually do only among relatively familiar and equal people.[1]

Such attitudes were not restricted solely to South Texas, nor were they confined to the 1920s, as a contemporary generation of Tejanos can attest. For in different parts of the states, and deep into the 1900s, Anglos were more or less still parroting the comments of their forbears.

Certain perceptions, however, did change over time—attitudes were not static; historical forces rarely are. Attitudes toward Mexican morality, for one, were no longer as indicting as they had been when Anglos met Mexicans in the decades before the Civil War. Whites no longer talked so loosely of Mexican voluptuousness, base immorality, and hot-constitutioned *señoritas*. In part that had to do with the fact that there was now an ample supply of Anglo women, so that there was less need for Tejanas as sexual partners for Anglo men; in part, with societal taboos putting an end to Tejano cultural traditions which Anglos had associated with vulgarity and with the fact that feelings about morality were expressed in more subtle and private ways.

Neither did every perception about race make it monolithically into the new century. The statements about Mexicans being physiologically similar to blacks and Indians and Tejanos being an aberration because of their degenerate parentage were no longer as vehement. Nor did whites think out loud about the depravity and savagery that they thought innate in Mexicans. But that reticence was indicative more of the institutionalization of that thinking than of its disappearance, for certain views Anglos expressed reflected much of the past. They regarded Mexicans as a colored people, discerned the Indian ancestry in them, and identified them socially with blacks. In principle and fact, Mexicans were regarded not as a nationality related to whites, but as a race apart.[2]

Given the persistence of those attitudes, and the corollary that Tejanos were a species of humanity different from (and inferior to) Anglos, it is not surprising to find violence still coloring relations between the two peoples. Texas Rangers, for one, continued to live up to the description given of them by nineteenth-century observers as a police body determined to keep the Mexicans down. In the 1910s, especially, they carried out a campaign of execution against Tejanos of South Texas on the pretext that they were trying to put an end to Mexican revolutionary raids in the region.[3] Their intimidation of Mexican Americans and violation of the Tejanos' civil rights by no means diminished after the Mexican Revolution.[4]

Self-proclaimed vengeance groups, meanwhile, assumed the task of avenging any offense against the white structure, just as in frontier days. A lynching party took Antonio Rodríguez from the

Rocksprings jail in November 1910 and burned him at the stake for allegedly killing a white woman. The next year, a group of men in Thorndale beat fourteen-year-old Antonio Gómez to death and dragged his body around town in reprisal for the murder of a Texas-German whom Gómez was accused of killing.[5] In 1922, similar cases of wanton murders occurred throughout the state.[6] Whether these cases signified the ending of an era of pathological violence against Tejanos remains to be documented, but as late as 1953, the town of Sonora in West Texas was the scene of the sadistic mutilation-murder of seventeen-year-old Raúl Arevalo, killed, according to those who talked of the case, for courting a local white girl.[7]

Anglo attitudes toward Tejano culture on the other hand, remained stable on the whole; remarkably similar, in fact, to the perceptions of the 1870s and 1880s. The same thing that Anglos had said about irresponsible Mexicans in South and West Texas who lived on nothing surfaced periodically after 1900; and, due to the belief that Mexican toil ought to be cheap, Tejanos were often paid less than Anglos who did the same work.[8] Further, Anglos insisted that Tejanos were culturally dissimilar from themselves and were thus unassimilable; that because of Mexican culture, the difficulties Tejanos faced were of their own making; and that Mexican Americans complacently accepted their fate of social inequality.[9] These views, most vociferously articulated by social scientists, have persisted to this day.[10] They remain as the most common attitudes about Mexicanos that the Anglo public clings to.

As to the Tejanos' Americanism, concern over it seems not to have equaled that of earlier times; perhaps because the old conditions that had wrought such accusations no longer prevailed in the twentieth century. Nonetheless, the experience of the Tejanos until recent years bespeaks a perception of them as a people not completely accepted as Americans. At least in two eras of heightened nativism, during the Depression of the 1930s[11] and the McCarthy years of the 1950s,[12] Mexican Americans have been subjected to harassment (and even repatriation) as if they were foreigners. Additionally, they have been regarded as alien in behavior; and thus white society has condoned the actions of such government agencies as the Border Patrol, which approaches Mexican Americans as if they are not Americans.[13] The educational system has historically been out to eradicate vestiges of un-Americanism and the notorious "no-Spanish rule" has ever admonished that "Americans speak English."[14]

Sometime in the fifteen years after World War II, attitudes to-

ward race, "depravity," loyalty, and other aspects of prejudice under-
went a visible change. In the late 1940s, according to the investiga-
tions carried out by Pauline Kibbe (*The Latin Americans of Texas*)
and Alonso Perales (*Are We Good Neighbors?*), Tejanos still faced an
Anglo world in many ways as hostile as that of the pre–World War II
years. But at the same time, the meaning of the war as a victory for
democracy and combined pressure from groups like the American
GI Forum and the NAACP were bringing about changes of perceptions toward ethnic minorities. To be sure, the 1950s were years of
repression, but simultaneously, government was pursuing a policy of
correcting past injustices. Legalized segregation ended, political
mechanisms designed to obstruct voting toppled, and it became un-
popular to be racist publicly. Attitudes die hard, of course, which is
why Chicanos came out in a full-scale movement in the 1960s and
1970s to demand of white society an end to notions that went back
for centuries.

If our times are compared with the nineteenth century, Anglo
Americans obviously do not regard Mexican Americans as they did
in the past. Closer contact between the two communities has tended
to dilute many of those attitudes. Still, many Anglos judge Mexican
Americans not by their character, but by the difference they see between themselves and Tejanos. Ideas that Mexican Americans are
culturally backward are a softer way of saying that they are racially
inferior. Though talk does not surface about Mexicans being a li-
bidinous people, off-color jokes about Chicano sexual incontinence,
for example, point starkly to the persistence of similar attitudes in a
more discreet form. Mexican Americans may no longer be suspected
of being un-American, but ethnic slurs and racial epithets carry connotations that they are far from being WASPs. And even if Tejanos
are no longer lynched, they are victims of psychological violence in
the more subtle forms of discrimination. Many of these views and
actions are predicated on the old notion that Tejanos are "not the
white man's equal."

Notes

Preface

1. Such works include Raymund Paredes, "The Image of the Mexican in American Literature" (Ph.D. dissertation, University of California, Berkeley, 1974); idem, "The Origins of Anti-Mexican Sentiment in the United States," in *New Directions in Chicano Scholarship*, ed. Ricardo Romo and Raymund Paredes, pp. 139–166; idem, "The Mexican Image in American Travel Literature," *New Mexico Historical Review* 52 (January 1977): 5–29; James Ernest Crisp, "Anglo-Texan Attitudes toward the Mexican, 1821–1845" (Ph.D. dissertation, Yale University, 1976); and Cecil Robinson, *Mexico and the Hispanic Southwest in American Literature.*

2. See, for example, Richard Drinnon, *Facing West: The Metaphysics of Indian Hating and Empire Building*, pp. xvi–xvii, 51; Ronald Sanders, *Lost Tribes and Promised Lands: The Origins of American Racism*, pp. 53–73; Richard S. Slotkin's review of Sanders' *Lost Tribes and Promised Lands*, in *New Republic*, May 6, 1978, pp. 25–28; and Thomas F. Gossett, *Race: The History of an Idea in America*, p. 3. For a somewhat different interpretation of those authors' argument, read George M. Frederickson, *White Supremacy: A Comparative Study in American and South African History* pp. 70, 73–74.

1. Initial Contacts: Redeeming Texas from Mexicans, 1821–1836

1. Seymour V. Connor, *Texas: A History*, p. 120.
2. Crisp, "Anglo-Texan Attitudes toward the Mexican," p. 5.
3. Select works advancing this argument include Ronald T. Takaki, *Iron Cages: Race and Culture in Nineteenth Century America*, pp. 11–15; Drinnon, *Facing West*, p. 465; Gary B. Nash, *Red, White, and Black: The Peoples of Early America*, 2d ed., pp. 81–82; David Brion Davis, *The Problem of Slavery in Western Culture*, p. 4; and Robert F. Berkhoffer, Jr., *The White Man's Indian: Images of the American Indian from Columbus to the Present*, p. 27. See also Bernard W. Sheehan, *Savagism and Civility: Indians and Englishmen in Colonial Virginia.*

4. Richard Slotkin, *Regeneration through Violence: The Mythology of the American Frontier, 1600–1860*, p. 5.

5. The same need to subjugate others at whatever cost would mold Anglo/Mexican relations after that and would continue westward to find further expression in California, in the "white man's burden" in the Pacific, and finally in Vietnam (Takaki, *Iron Cages*, p. xvii; Drinnon, *Facing West*, p. xvii).

6. Samuel H. Lowrie, *Culture Conflict in Texas, 1821–1836*, p. 68.

7. William H. Wharton, Address, April 26, 1836, in *The Papers of Mirabeau Buonaparte Lamar*, ed. Charles Adams Gulick, Jr., and Winnie Allen (cited hereafter as *Lamar Papers*), 1:365 (emphasis in original).

8. Stephen F. Austin to Thomas F. Leaming, July 23, 1831, in *The Austin Papers*, ed. Eugene C. Barker, 2:414, 427, 678.

9. Stephen F. Austin to Mrs. Mary Austin Holley, August 21, 1835, in *Austin Papers*, 3:101–103 (emphasis in original).

10. Cited by Mattie Alice Hatcher, *The Opening of Texas to Foreign Settlement, 1801–1821*, p. 277.

11. John William O'Neal, "Texas, 1791–1835: A Study in Manifest Destiny" (M.A. thesis, East Texas State University, 1969), pp. 90–93.

12. Paredes, "The Origins of Anti-Mexican Sentiment in the United States," pp. 139–166. Others supporting Paredes' position are S. Dale McLemore, "The Origins of Mexican American Subordination in Texas," *Social Science Quarterly* 53 (March 1973):663; David J. Weber, ed., *Foreigners in Their Native Land*, pp. 59–61, 89; and idem, "'Scarce More than Apes': Historical Roots of Anglo-American Stereotypes of Mexicans in the Border Region," in *New Spain's Far Northern Frontier: Essays on Spain in the American West, 1540–1821*, ed. David J. Weber, pp. 295–307.

13. Eugene C. Barker, *The Life of Stephen F. Austin: Founder of Texas, 1793–1836*, p. 149.

14. Andrew Anthony Tijerina, "Tejanos and Texas: The Native Mexicans of Texas, 1820–1850" (Ph.D. dissertation, University of Texas at Austin, 1977), pp. 10–14, 37–39, 44–45; Alicia V. Tjarks, "Comparative Demographic Analysis of Texas, 1777–1793," *Southwestern Historical Quarterly* 77 (January 1974):291–338.

15. William F. Gray, *From Virginia to Texas . . .* , p. 92.

16. J. C. Clopper, "Journal of J. C. Clopper, 1828," *Southwestern Historical Quarterly* 13 (July 1909):72, 76.

17. *Texian and Emigrant's Guide* (Nacogdoches), December 26, 1835, p. 4. See as well the *Telegraph and Texas Register* (San Felipe de Austin), January 23, 1836, pp. 102–103.

18. Quoted by Crisp, "Anglo-Texan Attitudes toward the Mexican," p. 22.

19. Clopper, "Journal," p. 76 (emphasis in original).

20. David Woodman, *Guide to Texas Emigrants*, p. 35.

21. Houston to Soldiers, January 15, 1836, in *The Papers of the Texas Revolution, 1835–1836*, gen. ed. John H. Jenkins, 4:30.

22. Ernest W. Winkler, ed., *Manuscript Letters and Documents of Early Texians, 1821–1845*, p. 32.
23. William B. Dewees, *Letters from an Early Settler of Texas*, p. 56.
24. Dr. John Beales' Journal, 1833, in William Kennedy, *Texas: The Rise, Progress, and Prospects of the Republic of Texas*, p. 396.
25. Joshua James and Alexander McCrae, *A Journal of a Tour in Texas*, p. 15. Emphasis is McCrae's. See also Dewees, *Letters from An Early Settler*, p. 57, for remarks on the Mexican passion for gambling.
26. Clopper, "Journal," pp. 71–72.
27. Gray, *From Virginia to Texas*, p. 89.
28. Houston to Soldiers, January 15, 1836, in *Papers of the Texas Revolution* 4:30.
29. Benjamin Lundy, *The Life, Travels, and Opinions of Benjamin Lundy*, p. 95.
30. Amos Andrew Parker, *Trip to the West and Texas*, p. 122; see also Asahel Langworthy, *A Visit to Texas*, p. 15.
31. *New Orleans Bee*, November 5, 1834, p. 2.
32. Thomas J. Green to the Friends of Liberty throughout the World, April 5, 1836, in *Lamar Papers* 1:348.
33. George W. Smyth, "The Autobiography of George W. Smyth," ed. Winnie Allen, *Southwestern Historical Quarterly* 36 (January 1933):202.
34. Langworthy, *Visit to Texas*, p. 217.
35. Clopper, "Journal," p. 72.
36. Ibid.
37. Ibid., pp. 72–73.
38. *New Orleans Bee*, November 5, 1834, p. 2.
39. William Barrett Travis, *The Diary of William Barrett Travis, August 30, 1833–June 26, 1834*, ed. Robert E. Davis, pp. 15, 68, 85, 91, 142, 154, 170. The Spanish verb *chingar* (to have sexual relations with) is Travis' own term.
40. James W. Fannin to J. W. Robinson, February 7, 1836, in *Official Correspondence of the Texan Revolution, 1835–1836*, ed. William C. Binkley, 1:402 (emphasis in original). See also R. C. Morris to J. W. Fannin, February 6, 1836, in ibid. 1:400; Council to the People of Texas, February 13, 1836, in ibid. 1:419.
41. John W. Hall to Public, February 1836 (?), in *Papers of the Texas Revolution* 4:470.
42. W. B. Travis to Henry Smith, February 12, 1836, in *Official Correspondence of the Texan Revolution* 1:416.
43. Thomas J. Green to the Friends of Liberty throughout the World, April 5, 1836, in *Lamar Papers* 1:348; David G. Burnet to Henry Raguet, April 7, 1836, in *Official Correspondence of the Texan Revolution* 2:602.
44. James Morgan to S. P. Carson, March 24, 1836, in *Official Correspondence of the Texan Revolution* 1:534.
45. Meeting at Brazoria, March 17, 1836, in *Lamar Papers* 1:345.
46. Creed Taylor, *Tall Men with Long Rifles*, narrated by James T. De Shields, p. 9.

47. Sion R. Bostick, "Reminiscences of Sion R. Bostick," *Quarterly of the Texas State Historical Association* 5 (October 1901):95.
48. Stephen F. Austin to Mary Austin Holley, August 21, 1835, in *Austin Papers* 3:101–103.
49. D. G. Burnet to Henry Clay, March 30, 1836, in *Official Correspondence of the Texan Revolution* 2:561.
50. "Compendium of the Early History of Texas," in *The Texas Almanac, 1857–1873,* comp. James M. Day, p. 180.

2. Niggers, Redskins, and Greasers: Tejano Mixed-Bloods in a White Racial State

1. Terry G. Jordan, "Population Origins in Texas, 1850," *Geographical Review* 59 (January 1969):86–88. See also Barnes F. Lathrop, *Migration into East Texas, 1835–1860: A Study from the United States Census,* pp. 34–58. Mississippi, Tennessee, Arkansas, Alabama, Missouri, and other Southern states contributed 53.7 percent of immigrants into Texas west of the Trinity River from 1845 to 1860, according to William Wilson White, "Migration into West Texas, 1845–1860" (M.A. thesis, University of Texas, 1948), p. 16. Seymour V. Connor, on the other hand, found the immigrants so heterogeneous that they did not typify either the Southern or frontier states. Europeans added a unique character of their own, according to this view (Connor, *Texas,* p. 174).
2. *Arkansas State Gazette* (Little Rock), September 19, 1837, p. 3.
3. Carl of Solms-Braunfels, *Texas, 1844–1845,* p. 46. Concerning explanations as to why Europeans reacted the way they did to Mexicans, see David J. Weber, "Here Rests Juan Espinosa: Toward a Clearer Look at the Image of the 'Indolent' Californios," *Western Historical Quarterly* 10 (January 1979):61–68.
4. Ferdinand Roemer, *Texas: With Particular Reference to German Immigration and the Physical Appearance of the Country,* trans. Oswald Mueller, pp. 11, 120; William A. McClintock, "Journal of a Trip through Texas and Northern Mexico in 1846–1847," *Southwestern Historical Quarterly* 34 (October 1930):142; Benjamin F. McIntyre, *Federals on the Frontier: The Diary of Benjamin F. McIntyre,* ed. Nannie M. Tilley, pp. 254, 261; [John and William Wright?], *Recollections of Western Texas, 1852–1855,* p. 30; Philip H. Sheridan, *Personal Memoirs of Philip H. Sheridan, General, United States Army* 1:33. A recent study that pursues this argument is Samuel J. Surace, "Achievement, Discrimination, and Mexican Americans," *Comparative Studies in Society and History* 24 (April 1982):321–329.
5. Gilbert D. Kingsbury, "Texas: The Rio Grande Valley: Cortina" (typescript, Kingsbury Papers, Barker Texas History Center, University of Texas Archives, Austin), p. 146.
6. *Texas State Gazette* (Austin), April 21, 1855, p. 4; *Nueces Valley Weekly* (Corpus Christi), January 10, 1858, p. 3; E. Kirby Smith, *To Mexico with Scott: Letters of E. Kirby Smith to His Wife,* ed. Emma Jerome Blackwood, p. 19.

7. George W. B. Evans, *Mexican Gold Trail*, ed. Glenn S. Dumke, p. 18; Andrew Forest Muir, ed., *Texas in 1837: An Anonymous Contemporary Narrative*, p. 102. Eliza Johnston (wife of Albert Sidney Johnston), living in Texas in 1856, did find at least one exception—a Mexican, who after being captured and raised as a Comanche warrior, had become Indian "on every essential except colour. He is fair with sandy hair and more like an Irishman than a Mexican" ("The Diary of Eliza [Mrs. Albert Sidney] Johnston," ed. Charles P. Roland and Richard C. Robbins, *Southwestern Historical Quarterly* 60 [April 1957]: 500).

8. McClintock, "Journal," p. 142. For other examples of observers seeing Mexicans as being dark-colored, see Federick Law Olmsted, *A Journey through Texas*, p. 79; Victor Bracht, *Texas in 1848*, trans. Charles Frank Schmidt, p. 74; Ashbel Smith, *Yellow Fever in Galveston, Republic of Texas, 1839*, ed. Chauncey D. Leake, p. 60; W. Eugene Hollon, *Beyond the Cross Timbers: The Travels of Randolph B. Marcy, 1812–1887*, p. 36.

9. Olmsted, *A Journey through Texas*, p. 161.

10. Winthrop D. Jordan, *White over Black: American Attitudes toward the Negro*, p. 241.

11. John D. Reid, *Reid's Tramp: Or, A Journal of the Incidents of Ten Months' Travel . . .*, p. 38; Albert D. Richardson, *Beyond the Mississippi: From the Great River to the Great Ocean . . . 1857–1867*, p. 239. There are, of course, several explanations of the origin of the word *greaser*. See Lloyd Lewis, *Captain Sam Grant*, p. 142; Américo Paredes, "On 'Gringo,' 'Greaser,' and Other Neighborly Names," in *Singers and Storytellers*, ed. Mody C. Boatright et al., pp. 285–290; Cecil Robinson, *Mexico and the Hispanic Southwest in American Literature*, pp. 38–39; *Daily Cosmopolitan* (Brownsville, Texas), July 23, 1884, p. 3. Whatever the origins, the word was used commonly in reference to Mexicans.

12. Muir, ed., *Texas in 1837*, p. 6.

13. Adolphus Sterne, *Hurrah for Texas! The Diary of Adolphus Sterne*, ed. Archie P. McDonald, p. 94.

14. McIntyre, *Federals on the Frontier*, p. 254.

15. Oscar M. Addison to His Brother, February 14, 1854, Brownsville, Texas, Addison Papers, Barker Texas History Center, University of Texas Archives, Austin.

16. John James Audubon, *The Life of John James Audubon, the Naturalist*, ed. Lucy Audubon, p. 410; Emanuel H. D. Domenech, *Missionary Adventures in Texas and Mexico: A Personal Narrative of Six Years' Sojourn in Those Regions*, p. 83. For a discussion of the psychological connection between color and dirt, see Joel Kovel, *White Racism: A Psychohistory*, pp. 81–92. Concerning the idea as applied to Africans by the English, see Jordan, *White over Black*, pp. 42, 257.

17. Thomas W. Coleman to William Harrison, April 23, 1849 (Thomas W. Coleman Letter), Barker Texas History Center, University of Texas Archives, Austin.

18. Olmsted, *Journey through Texas*, p. 454. In 1845, serious debate dealing with the Mexicans' color arose at the state constitutional convention. Some of the delegates protested that limiting citizenship and franchise to free "white" males might exclude Tejanos (Crisp, "Anglo-Texan Attitudes toward the Mexican," pp. 413–416). For another example in which whites questioned Mexicans' right to citizenship because of their color, see *Texas State Gazette*, April 21, 1855, p. 4.

19. Joseph Eve, "A Letter Book of Joseph Eve, United States Chargé d'Affaires to Texas," ed. Joseph Nance, *Southwestern Historical Quarterly* 43 (October 1939): 218; (April 1940): 494, 506, 510.

20. Francis S. Latham, *Travels in Texas, 1842*, ed. Gerald S. Pierce, p. 37. Teresa (Griffin) Vielé, an army wife at Fort Brown before the Civil War, referred to Brownsville as a "half-breed" town (*"Following the Drum": A Glimpse of Frontier Life*, p. 104).

21. A. B. Lawrence, *Texas in 1840, or the Emigrant's Guide to the New Republic*, p. 227; Roemer, *Texas*, p. 11; [Wright and Wright?], *Recollections of Western Texas*, p. 32; McIntyre, *Federals on the Frontier*, p. 254. Miscegenation produced curious side effects in Mexicans, according to popular lore. According to border resident Jane Cazneau, "the stoic Mexican, true to his Indian nature, endures suffering himself in silent, passive fortitude, and has no tenderness or sympathy for suffering or anything else" (*Eagle Pass: Or, Life on the Border*, p. 68; see also pp. 53, 70), while the German Ferdinand Roemer believed that Mexicans had somehow inherited the same inclination and skill for stealing horses as their Indian ancestors (*Texas*, p. 150).

22. *House Exec. Doc.* No. 135, 34th Cong., 1st Sess. (Ser. 861), 1: 68–70. For a similar discourse on ethnology, see Vielé, "*Following the Drum*," p. 158.

23. Whites continued to hold such beliefs into the twentieth century. The theory of inferiority as a result of racial mixing has even found its way into historiography, where it is especially reprehensible. Historians adversely influenced by this upbringing have all too often sought to pass off their findings as "objective" history. For examples in scholarly works, see Walter Prescott Webb, *The Texas Rangers: A Century of Frontier Defense*, p. 14, and the criticisms leveled at Webb by Américo Paredes, "*With His Pistol in His Hand*": *A Border Ballad and Its Hero*, p. 17. For another example, note Leonard Pitt, *The Decline of the Californios: A Social History of the Spanish-Speaking Californians, 1846–1890*, p. 16, and the charges directed at Pitt by Ray V. Padilla, "A Critique of Pittian History," *El Grito* 6 (Fall 1972): 20.

24. *Democratic Statesman* (Austin), December 9, 1873, p. 1; *San Antonio Herald*, January 17, 1871, p. 3. Concerning the word *Aztec* and its implications, more will be said in Chapter 6.

25. Harriet Spofford, "San Antonio de Béxar," *Harper's New Monthly Magazine* 55 (November 1877): 838.

26. Nathaniel A. Taylor, *The Coming Empire: Or, Two Thousand Miles in Texas on Horseback*, p. 106.

27. *San Angelo Standard*, September 21, 1889, p. 1 (reprinted from the *Chattanooga Times*). C. S. Phillips, a South Texas newspaperman, reported the poorer classes of San Diego, Texas, as looking very much like Choctaws in 1887 (*Beeville Bee*, May 19, 1887, p. 2).

28. Taylor, *The Coming Empire*, p. 106. Two writers for *Scribner's Monthly* repeated the impression of certain antebellum observers when they described the Mexicans of San Antonio in 1874 as a "bronzed" people (Edward King and J. Wells Champney, *Texas, 1874: An Eyewitness Account of Conditions in Post-Reconstruction Texas*, ed. Robert S. Gray, pp. 99, 100).

29. *San Angelo Standard*, September 21, 1889, p. 1.

30. Rudolf Eickemeyer, *Letters from the Southwest*, p. 14.

31. *Southern Intelligencer* (Austin) October 26, 1865. For the meaning of color in Elizabethan England, see Jordan, *White over Black*, p. 7. Roy Bedichek notes that racial prejudice, including certain values expressed in colors, has found its way into the naming of Texas fauna (*Adventures with a Texas Naturalist*, p. 196).

32. *San Antonio Herald*, November 15, 1868, p. 1.

33. *Brownsville Ranchero*, May 25, 1867, p. 2.

34. *San Antonio Express*, August 5, 1871, p. 2.

35. Ibid., November 9, 1891, p. 61.

36. *San Antonio Herald*, February 9, 1868, p. 3; Telamon Cuyler, "Telamon Cuyler's Diary: To Texas in 1888," ed. John Hammond Moore, *Southwestern Historical Quarterly* 70 (January 1967): 484; Johnathan Gilmer Speed, "The Hunt for Garza," *Harper's Weekly*, January 30, 1892, p. 103; Richard Harding Davis, "Our Troops on the Border," *Harper's Weekly*, March 26, 1892, p. 294; Arnoldo De Léon, *In re Ricardo Rodríguez: An Attempt at Chicano Disfranchisement in San Antonio, 1896–1897*.

37. The humorists Alexander E. Sweet and John Armoy Knox noted that Mexicans had the best teeth in the world due partly to their Indian descent (*On a Mexican Mustang through Texas*, p. 315).

38. Mary S. Helm, *Scraps of Early Texas History*, pp. 52–53. See also *San Antonio Express*, April 27, 1891, p. 4.

39. *San Antonio Express*, December 15, 1890, p. 4.

40. Editorial, "The Latin Races in America," *Southern Review* 9 (April 1871): 326. See also Charles A. Gardiner, "The Future of the Negro," *North American Review* 139 (July 1884): 80.

41. See for example *San Antonio Express*, February 24, 1889, p. 2; April 27, 1891, p. 4. See also *Daily Democratic Statesman* (Austin), January 9, 1876, p. 1, concerning the "Mixture of Races and Mental Character."

3. An Indolent People

1. Domenech, *Missionary Adventures*, pp. 254–255. Concerning explanations related to the perceptions of indolence, see Edmund S. Morgan, "The Labor Problem at Jamestown, 1602–1618," *American Historical Review* 76 (June 1971): 595–611; Weber, "'Scarce More than Apes,'" pp. 301–303; David J. Langum, "Californios and the Image of Indo-

lence," *Western Historical Quarterly* 9 (April 1978):181–196, and Weber's reply, "Here Rests Juan Espinosa." Other relevant studies include David Bertelson, *The Lazy South*, p. 75, and Herbert G. Gutman, "Work, Culture, and Society in Industrializing America," in *Work, Culture, and Society in Industrializing America*, ed. Gutman, pp. 3–78.

2. Olmsted, *Journey through Texas*, pp. 78–79, 151–152.
3. Cornelius C. Cox, "From Texas to California in 1849: Diary of C. C. Cox," ed. Mabelle Eppard Martin, *Southwestern Historical Quarterly* 29 (October 1925): 131.
4. Lawrence, *Texas in 1840*, p. 227; "Comanche Expedition, and a Glance at San Antonio, the Alamo, and the Dilapidated Missions [in 1840]," *Austin City Gazette*, June 10, 1840, as cited by Joseph Milton Nance, *Attack and Counter-Attack: The Texas-Mexican Frontier, 1842*, p. 454; Muir, ed., *Texas in 1837*, p. 101.
5. Muir, ed., *Texas in 1837*, p. 104. See also Olmsted, *Journey through Texas*, p. 160; Vielé, *"Following the Drum,"* p. 104.
6. William Russell Story, Diary, December 3, 1855–March 16, 1856, Barker Texas History Center, University of Texas Archives, Austin.
7. McIntyre, *Federals on the Frontier*, p. 262.
8. Lawrence, *Texas in 1840*, p. 227; Frederic Benjamin Page, *Prairiedom: Rambles and Scrambles in Texas . . .*, p. 127.
9. Vielé, *"Following the Drum,"* p. 104; Story, Diary.
10. John Russell Bartlett, *Personal Narrative of Explorations and Incidents in Texas, New Mexico, California, Sonora, and Chihuahua*, p. 40.
11. Page, *Prairiedom*, p. 128; Gray, *From Virginia to Texas*, p. 92; R. W. Johnson, *A Soldier's Reminiscences in Peace and War*, p. 67; *Galveston Weekly News*, May 15, 1855, p. 3; August 31, 1858, p. 1; Herman Ehrenberg, *With Milam and Fannin: Adventures of a German Boy in Texas' Revolution*, p. 105; *Texas State Gazette*, August 27, 1859, p. 2.
12. Muir, ed., *Texas in 1837*, p. 106; Solms-Braunfels, *Texas, 1844–1845*, p. 47.
13. Bracht, *Texas in 1848*, p. 68.
14. McClintock, "Journal," p. 144.
15. Richardson, *Beyond the Mississippi*, pp. 237–238.
16. H. H. McConnell, *Five Years a Cavalryman: Or, Sketches of Regular Life on the Texas Frontier, Twenty Odd Years Ago*, p. 188.
17. King and Champney, *Texas, 1874*, pp. 108–111.
18. James L. Rock and W. I. Smith, *Southern and Western Texas Guide for 1878*, pp. 166–167.
19. Frank H. Taylor, "Through Texas," *Harper's New Monthly Magazine* 59 (October 1879):712–713.
20. Quoted in *Victoria Advocate*, May 17, 1879, p. 2.
21. *San Antonio Express*, April 25, 1869, p. 1.
22. Reported in the *San Angelo Standard*, January 15, 1887, p. 4.
23. Lee C. Harby, "Texan Types and Contrasts," *Harper's New Monthly Magazine* 81 (July 1890):235.
24. *San Antonio Express*, November 10, 1880, p. 4.

25. William M. Pierson to Hon. Second Assistant Secretary of State, March 11, 1873, Despatches from United States Consuls in Ciudad Juárez (Paso del Norte), 1850–1906: January 16, 1871–December 31, 1884, General Records of the Department of State, Record Group 59, National Archives.

26. *El Paso Times*, June 6, 1897, p. 2.

27. *San Antonio Express*, October 7, 1879, p. 4; see also Mary A. Sutherland, *The Story of Corpus Christi*, ed. Frank B. Harrison, pp. 83–84.

28. *San Angelo Standard*, September 21, 1889, p. 1.

29. *El Paso Times*, August 21, 1883, p. 3; Alexander E. Sweet and John Armoy Knox, *Sketches from "Texas Siftings,"* pp. 55–57; Taylor, "Through Texas," pp. 712–713; Spofford, "San Antonio de Béxar," p. 838; Harby, "Texan Types and Contrasts," p. 244; *San Angelo Standard*, September 21, 1889, p. 1; *San Antonio Express*, February 21, 1886, p. 15.

30. Harby, "Texan Types and Contrasts," p. 244; see also Spofford, "San Antonio de Béxar," p. 838.

31. *Brownsville Ranchero*, November 18, 1866, p. 2; January 6, 1870, p. 2; Rock and Smith, *Southern and Western Texas Guide for 1878*, p. 133; *El Paso Herald*, September 13, 1882, p. 4; Stephen Powers, *Afoot and Alone: A Walk from Sea to Sea . . .* , p. 163.

32. *San Antonio Express*, June 17, 1886, p. 7; January 1, 1889, p. 7.

33. Sutherland, *The Story of Corpus Christi*, pp. 84–85.

34. *San Antonio Express*, March 12, 1879, p. 4. See also Max Krueger, *Pioneer Life in Texas*, p. 187; *San Angelo Standard*, September 28, 1889, p. 2.

35. W. M. Walton, *Life and Adventures of Ben Thompson: The Famous Texan*, p. 36. See also, for the impressions of an out-of-state journalist, Harby, "Texan Types and Contrasts," p. 245.

36. *El Paso Herald*, November 24, 1881, p. 1.

37. *San Antonio Express*, September 12, 1882, p. 2. For similar remarks about Rio Grande City, see the *Beeville Bee*, May 2, 1889, p. 1. For a reaction to women gambling, see *Corpus Christi Weekly Caller*, January 6, 1893, p. 7.

38. *El Paso Herald*, January 11, 1882, p. 4.

39. Sweet and Knox, *On a Mexican Mustang*, pp. 310–311. See further comments in the *San Antonio Express*, July 27, 1879, p. 4; January 15, 1888, p. 7.

40. *Beeville Bee*, January 20, 1899, p. 1.

41. *San Antonio Express*, December 3, 1879, p. 2.

42. Ibid., August 3, 1879, p. 4.

43. Ibid., November 10, 1880, p. 4. See also Sweet and Knox, *Sketches from "Texas Siftings,"* p. 91.

44. *San Antonio Express*, December 14, 1881, p. 1.

45. *Austin Statesman*, December 1, 1889, p. 7.

46. *El Paso Herald*, July 8, 1897, p. 2.

4. Defective Morality

1. Among the more recent writers to make this point is Berkhoffer, *The White Man's Indian*, pp. 25–31.
2. Jordan, *White over Black*, p. 579.
3. The concept of projection is used by both Berkhoffer, *The White Man's Indian*, and, Jordan, *White over Black*. David J. Weber explores briefly the idea of negative stereotypes being extended to Mexicans in the American Southwest in "'Scarce More than Apes,'" pp. 295–304.
4. J. W. Benedict, "Diary of a Campaign against the Comanches," ed. R. C. Clark, *Southwestern Historical Quarterly* 32 (April 1929): 305; Vielé, *"Following the Drum,"* p. 148. See also Robinson, *Mexico and the Hispanic Southwest in American Literature*, p. 82. One person who enjoyed the revelry of the *fandango* and the "accommodating" women partaking in it was Samuel E. Chamberlain, a soldier temporarily stationed in San Antonio before departing to fight in the Mexican War of 1846–1848 (Samuel E. Chamberlain, *My Confessions: The Recollections of a Rogue*, pp. 44–45).
5. Page, *Prairiedom*, pp. 42–44; William Bollaert, *William Bollaert's Texas*, ed. W. Eugene Hollon and Ruth Latham Butler, p. 218.
6. Muir, ed., *Texas in 1837*, p. 106; Roemer, *Texas*, p. 123.
7. George Wilkins Kendall, *Narrative of an Expedition across the Great Southwestern Prairies, from Texas to Santa Fe*, 1:48–49. For a reaction from a correspondent in Brownsville, see the *Galveston Weekly News*, August 31, 1858, p. 1.
8. R. H. Williams, *With the Border Ruffians: Memories of the Far West, 1852–1868*, ed. E. W. Williams, p. 177.
9. Muir, ed., *Texas in 1837*, p. 103.
10. Roemer, *Texas*, pp. 124–125.
11. Quoted by Sweet and Knox, *On a Mexican Mustang*, p. 309. A number of observers noted a certain Mexican love for the bath and swimming. For specific examples see Vielé, *"Following the Drum,"* p. 155; Olmsted, *Journey through Texas*, p. 157. Yet this did nothing to erase the image of the "dirty Mexican" reported in Chapter 2, reaffirming the premise that "filthiness" was associated with skin color rather than the actual condition of the Mexicans' bodies.
12. Muir, ed., *Texas in 1837*, p. 103.
13. Cox, "From Texas to California," p. 131.
14. Ehrenberg, *With Milam and Fannin*, p. 102; William E. Connelley, *Doniphan's Expedition and the Conquest of New Mexico and California*, pp. 387, 397; Reid, *Reid's Tramp*, p. 148; Johnson, *A Soldier's Reminiscences*, p. 67. See also Solms-Braunfels, *Texas*, p. 47; Bracht, *Texas in 1848*, p. 72; *Corpus Christi Ranchero*, March 16, 1861, p. 2.
15. "Comanche Expedition . . . ," *Austin City Gazette*, June 10, 1840, cited by Nance, *Attack and Counter-Attack*, pp. 454–455. See also McClintock, "Journal," pp. 142–143; Domenech, *Missionary Adventures*, p. 254.
16. Olmsted, *Journey through Texas*, pp. 151–152.

17. Latham, *Travels in Texas*, pp. 37–38 (emphasis in original).
18. McClintock, "Journal," pp. 142–143. See also W. S. Henry, *Campaign Sketches of the War with Mexico*, p. 25. For a poem entitled "The Daughter of Mendoza," and said to have been written by Mirabeau B. Lamar, one of the presidents of the Republic of Texas, see *Austin Statesman*, October 2, 1885, p. 2.
19. Jovita González, "Social Life in Cameron, Starr, and Zapata Counties" (M.A. thesis, University of Texas, 1930), pp. 26–27, 102, 105–106.
20. Aaron M. Boom, ed., "Texas in the 1850s, As Viewed by a Recent Arrival," *Southwestern Historical Quarterly* 70 (October 1966): 283.
21. Lawrence, *Texas in 1840*, p. 227.
22. Boom, ed., "Texas in the 1850s," p. 284.
23. Ibid.; Henry, *Campaign Sketches*, p. 26; Domenech, *Missionary Adventures*, p. 38; Evans, *Mexican Gold Trail*, p. 22.
24. Olmsted, *Journey through Texas*, pp. 162; 152.
25. McIntyre, *Federals on the Frontier*, pp. 272, 374.
26. Olmsted, *Journey through Texas*, p. 161.
27. Ibid., p. 161.
28. John C. Duval, *Early Times in Texas*, p. 41.
29. Reid, *Reid's Tramp*, p. 72. For more accounts, see John Salmon Ford, *Rip Ford's Texas*, ed. Stephen B. Oates, p. 62n, as taken from the *Texas Democrat* (Austin), September 16, 1847. See also *Arkansas State Gazette*, February 2, 1855; *Corpus Christi Ranchero*, March 16, 1861, p. 2.
30. Jane Dysart, "Mexican Women in San Antonio, 1830–1860: The Assimilation Process," *Western Historical Quarterly* 7 (October 1976): 365–375; Frank D. Bean and Benjamin S. Bradshaw, "Intermarriage between Persons of Spanish and Non-Spanish Surname: Changes from the Mid-Nineteenth to the Mid-Twentieth Century," *Social Science Quarterly* 51 (September 1970): 389–394; idem, "An Exploratory Study of Intermarriage between Mexican Americans and Anglo Americans, 1850–1960," *Southwestern Sociological Association Proceedings* (1970): 120–125; González, "Social Life in Cameron, Starr, and Zapata Counties," pp. 26–27, 102, 105–106; Carland Elaine Crook, "San Antonio, Texas, 1846–1861" (M.A. thesis, Rice University, 1964); *Arkansas State Gazette*, February 2, 1855; McIntyre, *Federals on the Frontier*, pp. 324–325; Connelley, *Doniphan's Expedition*, p. 397; *House Exec. Doc. No. 52*, 36th Cong., 1st Sess. (Ser. 1050), pp. 103–107; *House Exec. Doc. No. 81*, 36th Cong., 1st Sess. (Ser. 1056), p. 7.
31. Evans, *Mexican Gold Trail*, p. 22.
32. Richardson, *Beyond the Mississippi*, p. 238.
33. Jordan, *White over Black*, pp. 150–151.
34. *Brownsville Ranchero*, April 9, 1868, p. 2; July 29, 1868, p. 3; August 11, 1868, p. 3. See also *San Antonio Express*, October 4, 1892, p. 2.
35. *San Antonio Express*, April 19, 1874, p. 3.
36. *Brownsville Ranchero*, April 9, 1868, p. 2. Actually, as early as the 1850s, the city council had passed an ordinance prohibiting *fandangos*. Apparently, it was unenforceable. See James Robert Crews, "Reconstruc-

tion in Brownsville, Texas" (M.A. thesis, Texas Tech University, 1969), p. 28.

37. *San Antonio Herald*, November 26, 1872, p. 3.

38. *Democratic Statesman* (Austin), April 14, 1874, p. 2.

39. *San Antonio Express*, July 27, 1879, p. 4; August 5, 1879, p. 4. For a "typical scene" in San Antonio, see ibid., August 29, 1897, p. 12, covering "bawdy houses" on the city's West Side.

40. *Brownsville Ranchero*, August 25, 1868, p. 1; *San Antonio Express*, October 8, 1889, p. 3; August 13, 1893, p. 3.

41. *San Angelo Standard*, September 21, 1889, p. 1.

42. Ibid., September 23, 1889, p. 2.

43. Harby, "Texan Types and Contrasts," p. 239.

44. Ibid., p. 234. See also *San Antonio Herald*, August 16, 1868, p. 3; *Victoria Advocate*, April 2, 1887, p. 2; *San Antonio Express*, November 10, 1880, p. 4; Robert Maudslay, *Texas Sheepman: The Reminiscences of Robert Maudslay*, ed. Winifred Kupper, p. 123; Taylor, *The Coming Empire*, p. 107. For an example of the type of "Castilian" women that still appealed to Anglos in the postbellum period, see *San Antonio Express*, September 4, 1878, p. 3.

45. As reported in the *Corpus Christi Weekly Caller*, April 20, 1884, p. 2, from the *Louisville Courier & Journal*. Also published in *El Paso Herald*, August 17, 1884, p. 3, and *Austin Statesman*, April 16, 1884, p. 2.

46. *San Antonio Express*, April 5, 1883, p. 2. See also W. H. Chatfield, *The Twin Cities of the Border and the Country of the Lower Rio Grande*, p. 29; *San Antonio Express*, April 2, 1881, p. 1; January 15, 1888, p. 7; November 5, 1894, p. 2.

47. *San Antonio Herald*, May 25, 1868, p. 2.

48. See random examples in Jennie Parks Ringgold, *Frontier Days in the Southwest: Pioneer Days in Old Arizona*, pp. 8, 14; Will Hale [William Hale Stone], *Twenty Years à Cowboy and Ranchman in Southern Texas and Old Mexico: Desperate Fights with the Indians and Mexicans*, pp. 43–45, 11, 73, 136, 137; Anson Mills, *My Story*, ed. C. H. Claudy, p. 61; W. W. Mills, *Forty Years at El Paso, 1858–1898*, p. 176; Vinton Lee James, *Frontier and Pioneer: Recollections of Early Days in San Antonio and West Texas*, p. 73; Roscoe P. Conkling and Margaret B. Conkling, *The Butterfield Overland Mail, 1857–1869*, p. 81; *San Antonio Express*, January 24, 1883, p. 2; October 31, 1886, p. 2; November 9, 1886, p. 4; December 28, 1886, p. 4; June 7, 1888, p. 3; *Victoria Advocate*, November 24, 1877, p. 2. Secondary sources citing examples of mixed marriages include Leavitt Corning, *Baronial Forts of the Big Bend*, pp. 24, 45, 47, 58, and *A Twentieth Century History of Southwest Texas*. For cases involving Mexican men marrying Anglo women, see Ellis Arthur Davis, ed., *The Historical Encyclopedia of Texas*.

49. Napolean A. Jennings, *A Texas Ranger*, p. 16; Samuel Maverick, *Samuel Maverick, Texas, 1803–1870: A Collection of Letters, Journals and Memoirs*, ed. Mary Rowena Maverick Green, pp. 56, 110; Ford, *Rip*

Ford's Texas, p. 467; Sutherland, *Story of Corpus Christi,* p. 4; James, *Frontier and Pioneer,* p. 137; *Twentieth Century History of Southwest Texas; San Antonio Express,* October 7, 1879, p. 4; November 15, 1881, p. 1. And see especially Frederick Charles Chabot, *With the Makers of San Antonio: Genealogies of the Early Latin, Anglo-American, and German Families . . .*

5. Disloyalty and Subversion

1. Crisp, "Anglo Texas Attitudes toward the Mexican," pp. 91–92.
2. Ronnie C. Tyler, "Fugitive Slaves in Mexico," *Journal of Negro History* 57 (January 1972):2; Rosalie Schwartz, *Across the River to Freedom: U.S. Negroes in Mexico.* See also Paul S. Taylor, *An American Mexican Frontier: Nueces County, Texas,* pp. 33, 38.
3. Olmsted, *Journey through Texas,* pp. 65, 106, 163, 427.
4. *Texas State Gazette,* October 14, 1854, p. 4.
5. Ibid., September 9, 1854, p. 4; see also ibid., April 7, 1855, p. 2; October 14, 1854, p. 4; February 24, 1855, p. 4.
6. *Corpus Christi Ranchero,* March 17, 1860, p. 2.
7. Ibid., November 17, 1860, p. 2.
8. *Texas State Gazette,* September 2, 1854, p. 4; September 9, 1854, p. 5; *Galveston Weekly News,* September 5, 1854, p. 2.
9. As reported in the *Texas State Gazette,* February 24, 1855, p. 4.
10. Ibid., October 14, 1854, p. 4; November 4, 1854, p. 3; Olmsted, *Journey through Texas,* p. 235.
11. Olmsted, *Journey through Texas,* p. 164.
12. *Texas State Gazette,* October 14, 1854, p. 5. See also Paul D. Lack, "Slavery and Vigilantism in Austin, Texas, 1840–1860," *Southwestern Historical Quarterly* 85 (July 1891):1–20.
13. *Texas State Gazette,* October 21, 1854, p. 4; October 28, 1854, p. 4.
14. Olmsted, *Journey through Texas,* p. 164.
15. Ibid., p. 456. See also *Texas State Gazette,* April 7, 1855, p. 2; *Southern Intelligencer* (Austin), June 15, 1859, p. 2.
16. Extracts from the *Galveston News* and *True Issue,* in Olmsted, *Journey through Texas,* pp. 503–504. See also *Frank Leslie's Illustrated Newspaper* (New York), October 4, 1856, p. 260.
17. Extract from unidentified newspaper in Olmsted, *Journey through Texas,* p. 502.
18. Apparently first pointed out by *La Bandera Americana* of Brownsville, the Uvalde County resolutions were brought to the attention of Secretary of State Lewis Cass by the Mexican Minister in 1857. See the *San Antonio Herald,* November 28, 1857, p. 2. See also México, Comisión Pesquisidora de la Frontera del Norte, *Reports of the Committee of Investigation Sent in 1873 by the Mexican Government to the Frontier of Texas,* p. 129.
19. *San Antonio Herald,* August 14, 1855, p. 2; *Texas State Gazette,* November 15, 1856; *Southern Intelligencer,* December 17, 1856, p. 3; ex-

tracts from a Béxar Spanish-language newspaper in Olmsted, *Journey through Texas*, p. 514; Sister Paul of the Cross McGrath, *Political Nativism in Texas, 1825–1860*, pp. 103–104, 155–156.

20. *Austin State Times*, August 11, 1855, quoted by McGrath, *Political Nativism*, pp. 103–104; *San Antonio Herald*, August 14, 1855, pp. 2, 3; August 2, 1856, pp. 1, 2.

21. *House Exec. Doc.* No. 52, 36th Cong., 1st Sess. (Ser. 1050) (hereafter cited as *House Exec. Doc.* No. 52), pp. 70–72, 79–82. The literature on Juan Cortina himself remains weak and partisan and a definitive biography of the man is much needed. Traditional historians have portrayed him as a rogue, a bandit, a cattle rustler, and a "Red Robber." See for example, Rupert Richardson, Ernest Wallace, and Adrian Anderson, *Texas: The Lone Star State*, 3d ed., pp. 153, 255; Connor, *Texas*, pp. 237–238; Webb, *Texas Rangers*, pp. 175–193. Lyman Woodman, *Cortina: Rogue of the Rio Grande*, is similarly critical. Charles W. Goldfinch, *Juan Cortina, 1824–1892: A Re-appraisal*, and José T. Canales, *Juan N. Cortina Presents His Motion for a New Trial*, present him in a favorable light. In recent years, attempts have been made to interpret him as a social bandit conforming to the thesis advanced by J. Hobsbawm, *Primitive Rebels: Studies in Archaic Forms of Social Movements in the Nineteenth and Twentieth Centuries*. See in this respect Pedro Castillo and Albert Camarillo, eds., *Furia y muerte: Los bandidos chicanos*; Robert J. Rosenbaum, *Mexicano Resistance in the Southwest*, pp. 41–45, 52.

22. *House Report* No. 343, 44th Cong., 1st Sess. (Ser. 1709) (hereafter cited as *House Report* No. 343), pp. 116, 82.

23. *House Exec. Doc.* No. 52, p. 78. See also *Corpus Christi Ranchero*, January 5, 1861, p. 2.

24. *House Exec. Doc.* No. 52, pp. 32, 33, 48.

25. *House Exec. Doc.* No. 81, 36th Cong., 1st Sess. (Ser. 1056) (hereafter cited as *House Exec. Doc.* No. 81), p. 14.

26. *Corpus Christi Ranchero*, November 19, 1859, p. 2. Actually, these portrayals were unfounded. See James Leroy Evans, "The Indian Savage, the Mexican Bandit, the Chinese Heathen—Three Popular Stereotypes" (Ph.D. dissertation, University of Texas at Austin, 1967), pp. 117–135.

27. Jerry Don Thompson, *Vaqueros in Blue and Gray*, p. 81.

28. Quoted by Claude Elliot, "Union Sentiment in Texas, 1861–1865," *Southwestern Historical Quarterly* 50 (April 1947): 460–461.

29. *Corpus Christi Ranchero*, April 20, 1861, p. 2; April 27, 1861, p. 1; *Civilian and Gazette* (Galveston), May 7, 1861, p. 1; México, Comisión Pesquisidora . . . , *Reports of the Committee of Investigation*, p. 66.

30. *Galveston Weekly News*, December 23, 1863, p. 1. See also Taylor, *An American Mexican Frontier*, p. 47; Frank H. Smyrl, "Texans in the Union Army, 1861–1865," *Southwestern Historical Quarterly* 65 (October 1961): 245.

31. Among those who received the highest praises for their services to the

Confederacy were Santos, Refugio, and Cristóbal Benavides of Laredo. Their Civil War careers and their achievements are followed closely in Thompson, *Vaqueros in Blue and Gray*. Prominent examples of the praises given to these men may be found on pp. 14, 24, and 40 in Thompson's book.

32. Mills, *Forty Years at El Paso*, pp. 65, 99; *New York Times*, April 1, 1866, p. 1. The population figures, presumably, were the correspondent's own.

33. *Brownsville Ranchero*, July 2, 1867, p. 1.

34. Ibid., July 3, 1867, p. 2. See also February 25, 1868, p. 1; November 25, 1869, p. 2.

35. *San Antonio Express*, November 1, 1867, p. 2.

36. *San Antonio Herald*, February 5, 1868, p. 3. See also December 9, 1866, p. 2; December 27, 1866, p. 2; July 13, 1868, p. 3; May 27, 1868, p. 3.

37. Ibid., January 24, 1868, p. 3; February 9, 1868, p. 3; August 8, 1868, p. 2; *San Antonio Express*, February 8, 1868, p. 2.

38. *San Angelo Standard*, September 21, 1889, p. 1; *Corpus Christi Weekly Caller*, January 27, 1899, p. 1; *El Paso Times*, April 9, 1889, p. 1; April 10, 1889, p. 1; April 11, 1889, p. 4.

39. *El Paso Herald*, April 8, 1890, p. 1.

40. *San Antonio Express*, November 1, 1884, p. 1; *El Paso Times*, April 9, 1889, p. 1.

41. *Beeville Bee*, March 11, 1892, p. 2; *San Antonio Express*, November 1, 1884, p. 1.

42. Mexican Americans were not entirely passive subjects as Anglos contended. From the beginning of Anglo domination in 1836, Tejanos adjusted to the recent circumstances and sought participation in the new system. In areas where Tejanos were concentrated, numerous Mexican Americans served in office. At the local level, thus, Tejanos were able to have some degree of representation from office holders who were aware of the problems of their daily lives. Some of these Tejano politicians did turn to political bossism, but at times it was as a means to derive benefits from an Anglo political system reluctant to grant Tejanos constitutional privileges. Protest gatherings denouncing Anglo oppressors were not uncommon. For a fuller description of Tejano politics, see Arnoldo De León, *The Tejano Community, 1836–1900*, pp. 23–49.

43. *Corpus Christi Weekly Caller*, January 27, 1899, p. 1.

44. *New York Times*, August 28, 1880, p. 5; *San Antonio Express*, July 12, 1892, p. 6. See also *House Report* No. 343, p. 123; Speed, "The Hunt for Garza," p. 103.

45. *San Antonio Express*, December 14, 1881, p. 1.

46. Chatfield, *Twin Cities*, p. 29.

47. *El Paso Times*, July 22, 1886, p. 3.

48. *House Report* No. 343, p. 13.

49. *House Misc. Doc.* No. 64, 45th Cong., 2d Sess. (Ser. 1820) (hereafter cited as *House Misc. Doc.* No. 64), p. 261. See also *House Report* No. 343, p. 66.

50. *House Report* No. 343, p. 10.

51. *House Misc. Doc.* No. 64, pp. 107, 149; *House Report* No. 343, p. 7; *Nueces Valley Weekly*, August 22, 1874, p. 1.
52. *House Report* No. 343, p. 56.
53. Ibid., p. 77.
54. *San Antonio Express*, July 26, 1874, p. 3.
55. *Galveston Weekly News*, May 25, 1893, p. 6.
56. *San Antonio Express*, December 31, 1891, p. 2. See also *New York Times*, December 28, 1892, p. 5.
57. *New York Times*, April 28, 1898, p. 1. Rumors actually began in late March 1898. Suspicions that Spain intended to attack Texas developed when the mayor of Laredo allegedly received anonymous letters warning that his town would be razed, and when the Sheriff of Carrizo, R. A. Haynes, similarly received threats from suspected Spanish sympathizers in Mexico. Acting on tips from a friend in Mexico that Spanish supporters would cross the Rio Grande in late May, the sheriff of Laredo alerted Mexican authorities, who arrested the group. According to the *San Antonio Express*, the leader, Joaquín Martí, a native of Havana, Cuba, had arrived in Zapata County a year before and, with his second in command, a Dr. García, had thence crossed into Mexico, where, keeping in contact with officers in Havana, he prepared to cross the river simultaneously with the opening of hostilities between Spain and the United States. It was thought that a Washington Spanish attaché's trip to Mexico had been for the purpose of planning the possible strategy (*San Antonio Express*, March 31, 1898, p. 4). See further, Report from Consulate of the United States of America, Nuevo Laredo, Mexico, March 29, 1898, in Despatches from United States Consuls in Nuevo Laredo, Mexico, 1871–1906: July 3, 1893–July 30, 1906, General Records of the Department of State, Record Group 59, National Archives.
58. *San Antonio Express*, April 23, 1898, p. 8.
59. Ibid., April 27, 1898, p. 4. Like others before him, House stressed the theme that Mexicanos involved were "desperate characters and many of them refugees from justice." Some were troublemakers who had been recently expelled from Gonzales County, he said.
60. *Victoria Advocate*, April 30, 1898, p. 8.
61. *San Antonio Express*, April 27, 1898, p. 4; May 10, 1898, p. 3.
62. *Victoria Advocate*, April 30, 1898, p. 8. The Cinco de Mayo, a national holiday in Mexico, was traditionally celebrated in Mexican American communities in Texas. It commemorated the famous victory of General Ignacio Zaragosa over superior French forces attempting to conquer Mexico. The battle took place in Puebla, Mexico, on May 5, 1862.
63. *Beeville Bee*, April 29, 1898, p. 2. In San Antonio, the local Mexican American press was split on the issues concerning the fighting. *El Regidor* and *El Correo Mexicano* advanced the American cause, while *El Cronista* and *La Fe Católica* supported the Spanish cause. Alberto F. Martínez, a public school teacher in the city and the editor of *El Cronista*, was fired for his pro-Spanish sentiments. The mayor dismissed Martínez, upon learning of his ideas, with the statement: "This is an

American government and only Americans should be allowed to hold public offices." Martínez was also harassed by white juveniles for harboring Spanish sympathies (reported in the *San Antonio Express*, May 5, 1898, p. 6; May 6, 1898, p. 5; May 19, 1898, p. 5).

64. *Corpus Christi Weekly Caller*, April 15, 1898, p. 1; April 29, 1898, p. 1.

6. Leyendas Negras

1. Vielé, *"Following the Drum,"* p. 156.
2. As reprinted in the *San Antonio Express*, March 16, 1888, p. 7, under headlines "Bull Fighting in San Antonio—Scenes of San Pedro Park Thirty-Four Years Ago."
3. "Compendium of the Early History of Texas," in *Texas Almanac, 1857–1873*, comp. Day, pp. 116–117 (emphasis in original).
4. See Francis Latham's account of his emotional and spiritual purgation upon entering the Alamo six years after the battle there. To him, the adversaries had been a savage horde of barbarians (*Travels in Texas*, p. 34).
5. Muir, ed., *Texas in 1837*, pp. 102–103.
6. Olmsted, *Journey through Texas*, p. 159.
7. Muir, ed., *Texas in 1837*, p. 159.
8. Olmsted, *Journey through Texas*, p. 245. See also Melinda Rankin, *Twenty Years among the Mexicans: A Narrative of Missionary Labor*, p. 51.
9. John J. Linn, *Reminiscences of Fifty Years in Texas*, p. 264.
10. Quoted by Taylor, *Tall Men with Long Rifles*, p. 263 n. 3.
11. Noah Smithwick, *The Evolution of a State*, p. 131.
12. Samuel French, *Two Wars: An Autobiography*, p. 57.
13. *Galveston Weekly News*, August 14, 1855, p. 2.
14. *San Antonio Express*, April 18, 1869, p. 2. Few commented upon the Mexicans' Moorish and Arab past, but at least Captain John G. Bourke, a military man in Texas in the 1890s, found enough similarity in the lifestyle of Mexicanos in South Texas and Arabs to inspire him to write a lengthy essay, "Notes on the Language and Folk-Usage of the Rio Grande Valley," *Journal of American Folklore* 9 (April–June 1896): 81–116.
15. Walton, *Life and Adventures of Ben Thompson*, p. 45.
16. *San Antonio Express*, November 9, 1886, p. 5.
17. The list of references, mostly in newspapers of the era, is extensive. Twentieth-century writers explicitly maintained that the "cruel streak in the Mexican nature" was traceable to the Mexican Americans' Aztec Indian ancestry. See Webb, *Texas Rangers*, p. 14; Leo Grebler, Joan W. Moore, and Ralph Guzmán, *The Mexican American People: The Nation's Second Largest Minority*, pp. 529–530; Lieutenant Edward Duran Ayres' grand jury testimony on the criminal tendencies of Mexican American youths as reported in Matt Meier and Feliciano Rivera, eds., *Readings on La Raza: The Twentieth Century*, pp. 127–133. Armando Morales documents several expressions of these twentieth-century atti-

tudes in *Ando sangrando! I Am Bleeding*. A more recent work containing references to this perception is Surace, "Achievement, Discrimination, and Mexican Americans," p. 328.

18. *Beeville Bee*, May 2, 1889, p. 2.
19. *San Antonio Express*, January 9, 1885, p. 3. In Brownsville, the sport had been outlawed in the spring of 1857, though it probably continued clandestinely (Crews, "Reconstruction in Brownsville," p. 29).
20. *Brownsville Ranchero*, November 27, 1867, p. 2. Joseph G. McCoy, providing sketches of the cattle trade, agreed that Mexican *vaqueros* abused stock viciously. They had "no more feeling or care for brutes, either cattle or horses, than they had for stone," he noted, "and their heartless cruelty was proverbial." Not that they were incompetent, but unless their boss kept them under strict surveillance, he continued, they were "intolerably impudent and mean." The cattle driven by them were ordinarily "as poor as wood" (*Cattle Trade of the West and Southwest*, p. 86).
21. *San Antonio Express*, June 13, 1897, p. 1; June 25, 1897, p. 1.
22. Ibid., October 26, 1897, p. 2.
23. *Beeville Weekly Picayune*, May 26, 1899, p. 2.
24. *San Antonio Express*, May 1, 1891, p. 3.
25. Ibid., November 6, 1880, p. 3.
26. *Victoria Advocate*, September 29, 1877, p. 2.
27. *San Antonio Express*, July 18, 1879, p. 4.
28. *Austin Statesman*, January 3, 1885, p. 1. For a report of another such massacre, see *San Angelo Standard*, August 2, 1890, p. 2.
29. *San Antonio Express*, October 20, 1885, p. 1.
30. Speed, "The Hunt for Garza," p. 103. For further examples of reports concerning acts of special depravity among Mexicanos, who according to the *San Antonio Express* "had no proper conception of the heinousness of crime" (April 12, 1871, p. 4; see also January 13, 1883, p. 1; May 16, 1884, p. 1; May 21, 1884, p. 4; July 17, 1893, p. 5; July 18, 1897, p. 4).
31. *San Antonio Express*, February 2, 1875, p. 2.
32. Bob Kennon, *From the Pecos to the Powder: A Cowboy's Autobiography, As Told to Ramon F. Adams*, p. 30.
33. Susan G. Miller, *Sixty Years in the Nueces Valley, 1870–1930*, p. 106. See also Harby, "Texan Types and Contrasts," p. 234; *Corpus Christi Weekly Caller*, March 2, 1884, p. 4.
34. Harby, "Texan Types and Contrasts," p. 239. For an example of an attack upon such a stereotype, see the comments of a critic signing himself "Adios" in the *San Angelo Standard*, September 28, 1889, p. 2.
35. *San Antonio Herald*, July 26, 1874, p. 3.
36. *Corpus Christi Weekly Caller*, December 27, 1885, p. 1. When a Mexican was killed during a scuffle with a white man in the North Texas town of Cleburne, the *Austin Statesman* headlined the story "One Greaser Less" (May 27, 1893, p. 1).
37. Speed, "The Hunt for Garza," p. 103.

38. *San Antonio Express,* July 26, 1897, p. 8.
39. Maudslay, *Texas Sheepman,* p. 63. Jesse Sumpter, a citizen of Eagle Pass, related in his autobiography the story of a jury in deliberation trying to decide the fate of a Mexican murderer. Sumpter, who had witnessed the discussion as bailiff, said that when one member of the jury called for acquittal, another remarked: "No, we will not, we'll give him ten years in the penitent[i]ary, for he is a dam[n] Greaser anyhow." When the jury finally compromised by giving the defendant two years, Sumpter contemplated telling the judge of the deliberation. But, in the end, "I considered that it was better for that poor Mexican to go to the pentient[i]ary for two years, than it was for *me* to lose my life trying to defend him" (Jesse Sumpter, "Life of Jesse Sumpter: The Oldest Citizen of Eagle Pass, Texas," typewritten copy in Mary Couts Burnett Library, Texas Christian University, Fort Worth). For other accounts of Mexicans being regarded similarly, see the stories told to Florence Fenley in *Old Times: Their Own Stories,* pp. 44, 72.
40. Mary Jaques, *Texan Ranch Life, with Three Months' Travel through Mexico in a Prairie Schooner,* pp. 360–361. See also J. Marvin Hunter, *The Trail Drivers of Texas,* 2:664.
41. *Corpus Christi Weekly Caller,* November 30, 1884, p. 4.
42. Reprinted in *San Antonio Express,* August 29, 1886, p. 8.

7. Frontier "Democracy" and Tejanos—the Antebellum Period

1. Violence in Texas has been the subject of much attention by historians. Unfortunately, a good share of the writing is anecdotal, unanalytical, prosaic in its attention to feuds of various types, or romantic in its interpretation of gunslingers like John Wesley Hardin. Among the many such works is C. L. Sonnichsen's *Ten Texas Feuds.*

   The few studies that deal with violence toward the state's minorities are similarly shallow. Many issues are never addressed, especially in the cases of blacks and Mexican Americans. For example, what specifically was the motivation for violence against these two peoples? What segment of the white community was involved in the violence (or did Anglos participate in the violence monolithically), in what parts of the state, during which times, under what circumstances? Was violence primarily political, economic, psychological, racial, or class-based? Which elements within each of the respective minority communities were victimized especially—the poorer classes for the purpose of structuring a pliant labor force, the class of rising businesspeople and politicians who were seen as threats to the status quo, or all elements alike because of their ancestry?

   The underlying thesis advanced in Chapters 6–8 of this book is that Anglos saw Mexicans as part of a primitive state and dealt with them accordingly. This thesis borrows from the recent research on "regeneration through violence" and on "civilization" attempting to dominate "nature." Such an explanation is only one answer, however, and much more work remains to be done. Hopefully, this discussion will spur others to pursue those questions which might clarify the ambiguity of Anglo/Tejano violence in the nineteenth century.

2. John Pollard Gaines, "Diary of Major John Pollard Gaines of Kentucky, Volunteer Cavalry," ed. Dorman H. Winfrey, *Texana* (Winter 1963):35.
3. Chamberlain, *My Confessions*, p. 39.
4. Albert J. Myer, "I Am Already Quite a Texan: Albert J. Myer's Letters from Texas, 1854–1856," ed. David A. Clary, *Southwestern Historical Quarterly* 82 (July 1978):43.
5. Webb, *Texas Rangers*, p. ix. Webb's book has long been the standard work on the Rangers. For a new appraisal of the Rangers, see Julian Samora, Joe Bernal, and Albert Peña, *Gunpowder Justice: A Reassessment of the Texas Rangers*.
6. Fane Downs, "The History of Mexicans in Texas, 1820–1845" (Ph.D. dissertation, Texas Tech University, 1970), pp. 19–20.
7. Crisp, "Anglo-Texan Attitudes toward the Mexican," p. 342.
8. Roy Grimes, ed., *300 Years in Victoria County*, p. 458.
9. Tijerina, "Tejanos and Texas," p. 318.
10. *Lamar Papers*, 3:106–107.
11. Crisp, "Anglo-Texan Attitudes toward the Mexican," pp. 343, 384.
12. *Diamond Jubilee, 1847–1922, of the Diocese of Galveston and St. Mary's Cathedral*, compiled by the priests of the seminary, pp. 62–63.
13. Juan N. Seguín, *Personal Memoirs of John N. Seguín*, p. 19. Seguín's memoirs are reprinted in David J. Weber, ed., *Northern Mexico on the Eve of the United States Invasion*.
14. Gerald Pierce, "The Great Wolf Hunt: Tennessee Volunteers in Texas," *West Tennessee Historical Society Papers* 19 (1965):5–20.
15. Ilma M. Benavides, "General Adrian Woll's Invasion of San Antonio in 1842" (M.A. thesis, University of Texas, 1952), pp. 110–111, 114.
16. Harvey Alexander Adams, "Diary of Harvey Alexander Adams," typescript at Barker Texas History Center, University of Texas Archives, Austin, pp. 26, 3.
17. Sutherland, *Story of Corpus Christi*, p. 9.
18. Reprinted by *San Antonio Herald*, March 21, 1863, p. 2.
19. Olmsted, *Journey through Texas*, p. 164. The lynch law mentality came with the white pioneers of the 1820s, and thus serious talk of a lynching followed the attempted rape of a white woman by *presidio* soldiers in 1831. According to Texas Revolution veteran Creed Taylor, "as news of the affair spread, a posse gathered at the scene. All were highly wrought and some of them wanted to hang the wretch to the nearest limb; one or two suggested that the fiend's head be cut off and hoisted on a pole in view of the fort." Fearing that the lynching of a soldier in the Mexican Army would incur the wrath of the government, the party settled for a tar and feathering (Taylor, *Tall Men with Long Rifles*). There were four men attempting the rape; three escaped.
20. *Goliad Express*, as reprinted in the *San Antonio Herald*, August 18, 1857, p. 1.

21. Tucker Sutherland, "State of Texas Executed the First Woman in 1863," *San Angelo Standard-Times*, September 24, 1978, p. 1C.

22. Alfredo Mirandé and Evangelina Enríquez, *La Chicana: The Mexican American Woman*, pp. 69–71.

23. Olmsted, *Journey through Texas*, p. 164.

24. *Nueces Valley Weekly*, as reprinted in the *Galveston Weekly News*, January 31, 1854, p. 1.

25. *Texas State Gazette*, December 12, 1857, p. 1; *Southern Intelligencer*, September 9, 1857; September 23, 1857, p. 2; McGrath, *Political Nativism*, pp. 166–169. For a further account of the "Cart War," see Linn, *Reminiscences*, pp. 352–354; México, Comisión pesquisidora . . . *Reports of the Committee of Investigation*, p. 130.

26. *Texas State Gazette*, April 7, 1855, p. 4.

27. McGrath, *Political Nativism*, p. 167.

28. *Texas State Gazette*, December 12, 1857, p. 1; *Southern Intelligencer*, November 28, 1857; September 23, 1857, p. 2; McGrath, *Political Nativism*, p. 168.

29. *Southern Intelligencer*, September 9, 1857; September 23, 1857, p. 2. See also, relating to this economic concern, the *San Antonio Herald*, August 5, 1857, p. 2; August 6, 1857, p. 2; August 22, 1857, pp. 1, 2.

30. *Southern Intelligencer*, September 23, 1857, p. 2.

31. *Texas State Gazette*, August 15, 1857, p. 2. The *San Antonio Herald* was most emphatic in calling for some sort of way to bring about an end to the difficulties. See its August 5, 1857, issue, p. 2. But in Goliad County, where the outrages seemed to be at their worst, opposition to intervention was fierce, especially to one of a military kind. A concerned "Observer" who was seemingly indifferent to a racial clash between whites and Mexicans, did have reservations about a suppression of the perpetrators as it would certainly lead to a civil war among the Anglo-Saxon race (ibid., August 6, 1857, p. 2).

32. *Nueces Valley Weekly*, December 19, 1857, p. 2.

33. Robles y Pezuela informed Cass on October 14, 1857, of "extraordinary and atrocious" affairs taking place in Texas. According to Robles y Pezuela's sources, committees of armed men in the Béxar area had been organized for the purpose of hunting down Mexicans on the highways. Intent on despoiling the Mexicans of their property or killing them, whites had already killed seventy-five. Victims of these persecutions were arriving in Mexico to escape the wrath of the perpetrators. Exhorted by Robles y Pezuela to look into the matter, Cass urged Texas Governor Elisha M. Pease to act to suppress the troubles (*San Antonio Herald*, November 28, 1857, p. 2).

34. For the entire text of the resolutions which contained these remarks, see the *San Antonio Herald*, December 12, 1857, p. 2. See also *Nueces Valley Weekly*, January 10, 1858, p. 2.

35. *San Antonio Herald*, August 8, 1857, p. 2; McGrath, *Political Nativism*, pp. 167–168.

36. *House Exec. Doc. No. 52*, p. 33.

37. *House Report* No. 701, 45th Cong., 2d Sess. (Ser. 1824), p. v.
38. *Corpus Christi Ranchero*, November 26, 1859, p. 2.
39. *House Exec. Doc.* No. 52, p. 34.
40. Ibid., p. 39.
41. *Corpus Christi Ranchero*, November 12, 1859, p. 2.
42. Ibid., November 5, 1859, p. 2.
43. Ibid., December 17, 1859, p. 2; November 26, 1859, p. 2.
44. Contained in *House Exec. Doc.* No. 52, pp. 84–85.
45. Ibid., p. 50. See also *Corpus Christi Ranchero*, November 12, 1859, p. 2.
46. *House Exec. Doc.* No. 52, pp. 51, 58.
47. Ibid.
48. Ibid. *Corpus Christi Ranchero*, November 26, 1859, p. 2.
49. Ibid., November 12, 1859, p. 2.
50. Ibid., December 17, 1859, p. 2.
51. *House Exec. Doc.* No. 52, pp. 39, 51.
52. *Corpus Christi Ranchero*, January 28, 1860, p. 2.
53. *House Exec. Doc.* No. 52, pp. 58–60; *House Exec. Doc.* No. 81, p. 2. See also Evans, "The Indian Savage, the Mexican Bandit, the Chinese Heathen," pp. 117–135.
54. *Corpus Christi Ranchero*, November 15, 1859, p. 2.
55. Ibid., November 19, 1859, p. 2; January 28, 1860, p. 2.
56. Pierre Fourier Parisot, O.M.I., *The Reminiscences of a Texas Missionary*, pp. 99–100.

8. Frontier "Democracy" and Tejanos—the Postbellum Period

1. Richard Maxwell Brown, *Strains of Violence: Historical Studies of American Violence and Vigilantism*, pp. 237–238.
2. *House Misc. Doc.* No. 64, p. 230. Ben Kinchlow, an ex-slave who had at one time scouted for the Rangers, related the following story. As he and the Rangers sought to track down Mexican cattle rustlers near Brownsville during this period: "While we was eatin', we heard somebody holler, and he said, 'Boys, there they are!' And he said to me, 'Ben, you want to stay with the horses or be in the fun?' And I said, 'I don't care!' So he said, 'You better stay with the horses; you ain't paid to kill Meskins.' I went out to where the horses were. The rangers were afoot in the brush. . . . After the fight, the cap'n says to the boys, 'Well, boys, the fun is all over now, I guess we'd better start back to camp.' And they all mounted their horses and begun singin':

> O, bury me not on the lone prairie-e-e
> Where the wild coyotes will howl o'er me-e-e
> Right where all the Meskins ought to be-e-e."

(As related in George P. Rawick, ed., *Texas Narratives*, Parts 1 and 2, pp. 282–284.)
3. Jennings, *A Texas Ranger*, pp. 71–72. For a further description of the Rangers on the Nueces Strip, see James H. Cook, *Fifty Years on the Old Frontier*, pp. 95–100.

4. Frederic Remington, *Crooked Trails*, pp. 12–13, 16. *La ley de fuga* ("law of escape") was the frontier rule that justified killing an escaping prisoner.

5. A. J. Sowell, *Early Settlers and Indian Fighters of the Southwest*, 2:754. See also *San Antonio Herald*, September 20, 1868, p. 2; October 15, 1868, p. 2.

6. *San Antonio Express*, June 12, 1874, p. 2; June 13, 1874, p. 2; June 14, 1874, p. 2; June 16, 1874, p. 2. See also Hobart Huson, *Refugio: A Comprehensive History*, 2:206–210.

7. *House Misc. Doc.* No. 64, p. 230.

8. Carlysle Graham Raht, *The Romance of Davis Mountains and Big Bend Country*, pp. 304–305.

9. *San Antonio Express*, April 28, 1886, p. 4; April 29, 1886, p. 4; May 2, 1886, p. 4; *Corpus Christi Weekly Caller*, May 2, 1886, p. 8.

10. *Corpus Christi Weekly Caller*, May 9, 1886, p. 5.

11. *San Antonio Express*, June 30, 1896, p. 5.

12. As reported by Frank C. Pierce, *A Brief History of the Lower Rio Grande Valley*, p. 118.

13. Sumpter, *Life of Jesse Sumpter*, pp. 52–54.

14. *San Antonio Express*, October 8, 1895, p. 5; October 13, 1895, p. 3. See further Consulate General, Nuevo Laredo, Mexico, to Hon. William R. Day, Assistant Secretary of State, September 13, 1897, in Despatches from United States Consuls in Nuevo Laredo, 1871–1906.

15. *San Antonio Express*, January 31, 1896, p. 8.

16. *San Antonio Express*, April 20, 1886, p. 4; *San Angelo Standard*, April 24, 1886, p. 2; *Austin Statesman*, April 20, 1886, p. 1.

17. *San Antonio Express*, September 7, 1886, p. 4.

18. Seb S. Wilcox, "The Laredo City Election and Riot of April, 1886," *Southwestern Historical Quarterly* 45 (July 1941): 1–23; Sowell, *Early Settlers and Indian Fighters*, 2:630–633. The newspapers of the time all gave the incident full coverage. See especially the *San Antonio Express*.

19. According to the account printed in the *San Antonio Express*, Garza initiated the fight as Sebree defended himself (September 26, 1888, p. 4). Garza survived and later launched the invasion of Mexico discussed in Chapter 5.

20. Chatfield, *Twin Cities*, p. 43; *Beeville Bee*, September 27, 1888, p. 2; *New York Times*, September 29, 1888, p. 4; *San Antonio Express*, September 22, 1888, p. 4; September 24, 1888, p. 1; September 26, 1888, p. 4; September 27, 1888, p. 1; September 28, 1888, p. 1.

21. *Beeville Bee*, August 17, 1894, p. 7. See in addition demographic statistics for Bee County in ibid., June 7, 1888, p. 1.

22. *Beeville Bee*, March 24, 1899, p. 1; *San Antonio Express*, March 21, 1899, p. 1; March 22, 1899, p. 1; Albert Bigelow Paine, *Captain Bill McDonald, Texas Ranger*, p. 406; Sowell, *Early Settlers and Indian Fighters*, 2:630–632. See also *Corpus Christi Weekly Caller*, March 17, 1899,

p. 2, for the full text of the order placing Webb and Encinal Counties under smallpox quarantine. Especially directed toward Mexicanos, its purpose was to prevent cotton pickers with the disease from migrating into the interior of the state from the border areas.

23. *New York Times,* July 2, 1892, p. 1; *Austin Statesman,* July 2, 1892, p. 1; September 15, 1892, p. 1.
24. *Victoria Advocate,* December 29, 1877, p. 1.
25. Ibid., November 24, 1877, p. 2, as taken from a grand jury report investigating the recent number of killings taking place in Nueces County. See also *House Report* No. 343, pp. 7, 122.
26. *Austin Statesman,* June 27, 1874, p. 2.
27. *House Misc. Doc.* No. 64, p. 83. See also *House Report* No. 343, p. 149.
28. *House Report* No. 343, p. 56.
29. Ibid., p. 149; *Nueces Valley Weekly,* March 16, 1872, p. 2.
30. *San Antonio Herald,* March 16, 1870, p. 3; Williams, *With the Border Ruffians,* p. 176; *San Antonio Express,* June 21, 1875, p. 2; August 29, 1886, p. 8; *Brownsville Ranchero,* November 25, 1869, p. 2; February 10, 1872 (as reported in México, Comisión Pesquisidora . . . , *Reports of the Committee of Investigation,* p. 108); *House Report* No. 343, pp. 122, 124; *House Misc. Doc.* No. 64, p. 285.
31. Letter of J. L. Hall, Rio Grande City, September 15, 1877, to Hon. William Steele, Adjt. Gen., in Texas Adjutant General, Miscellany, 1839–1879, Barker Texas History Center, University of Texas Archives, Austin.
32. As reported in the *Brownsville Ranchero,* November 30, 1869, p. 1. The *Ranchero,* on p. 2 of the same edition, denied the veracity of the *Revista's* claim. See also *House Misc. Doc.* No. 64, p. 273; *San Antonio Express,* February 2, 1875, p. 2. See the *Express,* August 27, 1872, p. 1, for a response from a Tejano inveighing against the outrages of the 1870s.
33. *New York Times,* October 22, 1877, p. 2.
34. *Nueces Valley Weekly,* January 27, 1872, p. 2.
35. Ibid., August 24, 1872, p. 2.
36. Ibid., November 7, 1874, p. 3. "Texans are worth nothing as far as I'm concerned and this [killing one of them] makes very little difference to me." Both the paper and Paul S. Taylor (*American Mexican Frontier,* p. 59) interpreted this as a threat to kill the store owner.
37. William M. Hager, "The Nueces Town Raid of 1875: A Border Incident," *Arizona and the West* 1 (Spring 1959):258–270.
38. Jennings, *A Texas Ranger,* p. 130.
39. *House Report* No. 343, p. 124. See also Letter of Capt. L. H. McNelly, Rancho Santa Gertrudes, April 29, 1875, to Hon. William Steele, Adjt. Gen., in Texas Adjutant General, Miscellany, 1839–1879.
40. *House Report* No. 343, p. 57; *San Antonio Herald,* May 12, 1875, p. 1. The Encinal County mentioned was created on February 1, 1856, but was never organized. It was abolished on March 12, 1899, and the terri-

tory was incorporated into Webb County, according to *The Handbook of Texas* (Austin: Texas State Historical Association, 1952), 1:567.

41. Unless otherwise stated, material on the El Paso Salt War derives from *House Exec. Doc.* No. 93, 45th Cong., 2d Sess. (Ser. 1809). One of the better descriptive works on the Salt War is Sonnichsen, *Ten Texas Feuds*, pp. 108–156.

42. *San Antonio Express*, February 28, 1892, p. 6.

43. Ibid., April 16, 1892 Sección en Castellaño, pp. 1, 3. For an appeal by 125 Mexican American women to President Benjamin Harrison for his intercession in bringing relief to Tejanos in the beleaguered region, see *Corpus Christi Weekly Caller*, August 12, 1892, p. 1.

44. *Corpus Christi Weekly Caller*, November 18, 1892, p. 1.

45. *San Antonio Express*, August 9, 1892, p. 3.

46. *Austin Statesman*, September 22, 1892, p. 1.

47. *San Antonio Express*, December 28, 1897, p. 1; April 28, 1898, p. 5.

9. Epilogue: "Not the White Man's Equal"

1. Douglas E. Foley et al., *From Peones to Politicos: Ethnic Relations in a South Texas Town, 1900 to 1977*, pp. 43–44.

2. Taylor, *American Mexican Frontier*, pp. 203, 219, 295–297, and Chapter 20; William Madsen, *Mexican Americans of South Texas*, 2d ed., p. 13. See also Surace, "Achievement, Discrimination, and Mexican Americans," pp. 321–322.

3. Paredes, *"With His Pistol in His Hand,"* pp. 23–32.

4. Samora, Bernal, and Peña, *Gunpowder Justice*.

5. José Limón, "El Primer Congreso Mexicanista de 1911: A Precursor to Contemporary Chicanismo," *Aztlán: Chicano Journal of the Social Sciences and the Arts* 5 (Spring and Fall 1974):88.

6. *San Angelo Standard-Times*, November 15, 1922, p. 1; November 19, 1922, p. 1.

7. Ibid., March 2, 1953, p. 1. Also, oral interviews with citizens of Sonora, who prefer anonymity.

8. Taylor, *American Mexican Frontier*, p. 139; David Montejano, *Race, Labor Repression, and Capitalist Agriculture: Notes from South Texas, 1920–1930*, p. 20; Mario Barrera, *Race and Class in the Southwest: A Theory of Racial Inequality*, p. 78.

9. Madsen, *Mexican Americans of South Texas*, p. 14; Taylor, *American Mexican Frontier*, pp. 127, 128, 305.

10. Nick Vaca, "The Mexican American in the Social Sciences," *El Grito: A Journal of Contemporary Mexican American Thought* 3 (Spring 1970):3–24; 4 (Fall 1970):17–51.

11. Andrés A. Tijerina, *The History of Mexican Americans in Lubbock County*, p. 32; Abraham Hoffman, *Unwanted Mexican Americans in the Great Depression: Repatriation Pressures, 1929–1939*, p. 118; Lawrence A. Cardoso, *Mexican Emigration to the United States, 1897–1931*, p. 149.

12. Juan Ramón García, *Operation Wetback: The Mass Deportation of Mexican Undocumented Workers in 1954*, pp. 216, 218.
13. Grebler, Moore, and Guzmán, *Mexican American People*, pp. 535–536, 514.
14. Mario T. García, *Desert Immigrants: The Mexicans of El Paso, 1880–1920*, pp. 110–126; Thomas P. Carter, *Mexican Americans in School: A History of Educational Neglect*, pp. 9–18, 97–98.

Bibliography

PRIMARY SOURCES

U.S. Government Documents

Despatches from United States Consuls in Ciudad Juárez (Paso del Norte),
1850–1906: January 16, 1871–December 31, 1884. General Records of
the Department of State, Record Group 59, National Archives.

Despatches from United States Consuls in Nuevo Laredo, 1871–1906:
July 3, 1893–July 30, 1906. General Records of the Department of State,
Record Group 59, National Archives.

House Exec. Doc. No. 52, 36th Cong., 1st Sess. (Ser. 1050).

House Exec. Doc. No. 81, 36th Cong., 1st Sess. (Ser. 1056).

House Exec. Doc. No. 93, 45th Cong., 2d Sess. (Ser. 1809).

House Exec. Doc. No. 135, 34th Cong., 1st Sess. (Ser. 861). 2 vols.

House Misc. Doc. No. 64, 45th Cong., 2d Sess. (Ser. 1820).

House Report No. 343, 44th Cong., 1st Sess. (Ser. 1709).

House Report No. 701, 45th Cong., 2d Sess. (Ser. 1824).

Manuscripts

Adams, Harvey Alexander. "Diary of Harvey Alexander Adams." Typescript
at Eugene C. Barker Texas History Center, University of Texas Archives, Austin.

Addison, Oscar M. Oscar M. Addison Papers, 1834–1909. Eugene C. Barker
Texas History Center, University of Texas Archives, Austin.

Coleman, Thomas W. Letter, 1849. Eugene C. Barker Texas History Center,
University of Texas Archives, Austin.

Kingsbury, Gilbert D. "Texas: The Rio Grande Valley: Cortina." Typescript
in Gilbert D. Kingsbury Papers, 1855–1874, Eugene C. Barker Texas
History Center, University of Texas Archives, Austin.

Robertson, George L. George L. Robertson Papers, 1839–1869. Eugene C.
Barker Texas History Center, University of Texas Archives, Austin.

Story, William Russell. Diary, December 3, 1855–March 16, 1856. Eugene C. Barker Texas History Center, University of Texas Archives,
Austin.

Sumpter, Jesse. "Life of Jesse Sumpter: The Oldest Citizen of Eagle Pass, Texas." Typewritten copy in Mary Couts Burnett Library, Texas Christian University, Fort Worth.

Texas Adjutant General. Miscellany, 1839–1879. Eugene C. Barker Texas History Center, University of Texas Archives, Austin.

Newspapers .

Arkansas State Gazette (Little Rock). 1821–1837, 1855.
Austin Statesman. 1871–1899.
Beeville Bee. 1886–1900.
Beeville Weekly Picayune. 1892, 1894–1900.
Brownsville Ranchero. 1864–1870.
Civilian and Gazette (Galveston). 1861.
Corpus Christi Ranchero. 1859–1863.
Corpus Christi Weekly Caller. 1883–1889, 1891–1893, 1898–1900.
Daily Cosmopolitan (Brownsville). 1881, 1883–1885, 1892.
Daily Democratic Statesman (Austin). 1876.
Democratic Statesman (Austin). 1873–1874.
El Paso Herald. 1881–1899.
El Paso Times. 1883–1899.
Frank Leslie's Illustrated Newspaper (New York). 1856.
Galveston Weekly News. 1848–1858, 1862–1863, 1873, 1892–1893.
New Orleans Bee. 1834.
New York Times. 1866, 1874, 1877, 1888, 1892, 1898.
Nueces Valley Weekly (Corpus Christi). 1857–1858, 1870–1872, 1874.
San Angelo Standard. 1884–1900.
San Angelo Standard-Times. 1922, 1953, 1978.
San Antonio Express. 1865–1900.
San Antonio Herald. 1855–1878.
Southern Intelligencer (Austin). 1856–1861, 1865.
Telegraph and Texas Register (San Felipe de Austin). 1836.
Texas State Gazette (Austin). 1849–1860.
Texian and Emigrant's Guide (Nacogdoches). 1835.
Victoria Advocate. 1877–1900.

Books

Audubon, John James. *The Life of John James Audubon, the Naturalist.* Edited by Lucy Audubon. New York: G. P. Putnam's Sons, 1902.
Austin, Stephen F., et al. *The Austin Papers.* Edited by Eugene C. Barker. Vols. 1–2, Washington, D.C.: American Historical Association, 1924–1928; vol. 3, Austin: University of Texas, 1926.
Bartlett, John Russell. *Personal Narrative of Exploration and Incidents in Texas, New Mexico, California, Sonora, and Chihuahua.* New York: D. Appleton & Co., 1854.
Binkley, William C., ed. *Official Correspondence of the Texan Revolution, 1835–1836.* 2 vols. New York: D. Appleton-Century Company, 1936.
Bollaert, William. *William Bollaert's Texas.* Edited by W. Eugene Hollon and

Ruth Latham Butler. Norman: University of Oklahoma Press, 1956.

Bracht, Victor. *Texas in 1848*. Translated by Charles Frank Schmidt. San Antonio: Naylor Co., 1931.

Cazneau, Jane. *Eagle Pass: Or, Life on the Border*. Austin: Pemberton Press, 1966.

Chamberlain, Samuel E. *My Confessions: The Recollections of a Rogue*. New York: Harper and Brothers, 1956.

Chatfield, W. H. *The Twin Cities of the Border and the Country of the Lower Rio Grande*. New Orleans: E. P. Brandao, 1893.

Conkling, Roscoe P., and Margaret B. Conkling. *The Butterfield Overland Mail, 1857–1869*. Glendale: Arthur H. Clark Co., 1947.

Connelley, William E. *Doniphan's Expedition and the Conquest of New Mexico and California*. Kansas City: Bryant & Douglas Book and Stationery Co., 1907.

Cook, James H. *Fifty Years on the Old Frontier, as Cowboy, Hunter, Guide, Scout, and Ranchman*. Norman: University of Oklahoma Press, 1957.

Day, James M., compiler. *The Texas Almanac, 1857–1873*. Waco: Texian Press, 1967.

Dewees, William B. *Letters from an Early Settler of Texas*. Waco: Texian Press, 1968.

Domenech, Emanuel H. D. *Missionary Adventures in Texas and Mexico: A Personal Narrative of Six Years' Sojourn in Those Regions*. London: Longman, Brown, Green, Longmans, and Roberts, 1858.

Duval, John C. *Early Times in Texas*. Dallas: Tardy Publications, 1936.

Ehrenberg, Herman. *With Milam and Fannin: Adventures of a German Boy in Texas' Revolution*. Austin: Pemberton Press, 1968.

Eickemeyer, Rudolf. *Letters from the Southwest*. New York: Press of J. J. Little and Co., 1894.

Evans, George W. B. *Mexican Gold Trail*. Edited by Glenn S. Dumke. San Marino, Calif.: Huntington Library, 1945.

Ford, John Salmon. *Rip Ford's Texas*. Edited by Stephen B. Oates. Austin: University of Texas Press, 1963.

French, Samuel. *Two Wars: An Autobiography*. Nashville, Tenn.: Confederate Veterans, 1901.

Gray, William F. *From Virginia to Texas . . .* Houston: Fletcher Young Publishing Co., 1965.

Hale, Will [William Hale Stone]. *Twenty Years a Cowboy and Ranchman in Southern Texas and Old Mexico: Desperate Fights with the Indians and Mexicans*. Introduction by A. M. Gibson. Norman: University of Oklahoma Press, 1959.

Helm, Mary S. *Scraps of Early Texas History*. Austin: Printed for the author at the office of B. R. Warner and Co., 1884.

Henry, W. S. *Campaign Sketches of the War with Mexico*. New York: Arno Press, 1973.

James, Joshua, and Alexander McCrae. *A Journal of a Tour in Texas: With Observations, &c., by the Agents of the Wilmington Emigrating Society*. Wilmington, N.C.: Printed by T. Loring, 1835.

James, Vinton Lee. *Frontier and Pioneer: Recollections of Early Days in San Antonio and West Texas.* San Antonio: Artes Gráficas, 1938.

Jaques, Mary. *Texan Ranch Life, with Three Months Travel through Mexico in a Prairie Schooner.* London: Horace Cox, 1894.

Jenkins, John H., gen. ed. *The Papers of the Texas Revolution, 1835–1836.* 10 vols. Austin: Presidial Press, 1973.

Jennings, Napoleon A. *A Texas Ranger.* New York: Charles Scribner's Sons, 1899. Facsimile reproduction, Ruidoso, N.M.: Frontier Co., 1960.

Johnson, R. W. *A Soldier's Reminiscences in Peace and War.* Philadelphia: J. B. Lippincott Co., 1886.

Kendall, George Wilkins. *Narrative of an Expedition across the Great Southwestern Prairies, from Texas to Santa Fe.* 2 vols. London: David Bogue, 1845.

Kennedy, William. *Texas: The Rise, Progress, and Prospects of the Republic of Texas.* Fort Worth: Molyneaux Craftsmen, 1925.

Kennon, Bob. *From the Pecos to the Powder: A Cowboy's Autobiography.* As told to Ramon F. Adams. Norman: University of Oklahoma Press, 1965.

King, Edward, and J. Wells Champney. *Texas, 1874: An Eyewitness Account of Conditions in Post-Reconstruction Texas.* Edited by Robert S. Gray. Houston: Cordovan Press, 1974.

Krueger, Max. *Pioneer Life in Texas: An Autobiography.* San Antonio: Press of the Clegg Co., 1930(?).

Lamar, Mirabeau B. *The Papers of Mirabeau Buonaparte Lamar.* Edited by Charles Adams Gulick, Jr., and Winnie Allen. 6 vols. New York: AMS Press, 1973.

Langworthy, Asahel. *A Visit to Texas: Being the Journal of a Traveller through Those Parts Most Interesting to Settlers.* New York: Goodrich and Wiley, 1834.

Latham, Francis S. *Travels in Texas, 1842.* Edited by Gerald S. Pierce. Austin: Encino Press, 1971.

Lawrence, A. B. *Texas in 1840, or the Emigrant's Guide to the New Republic: Being the Result of Observation, Enquiry and Travels in the Beautiful Country.* New York: William W. Allen, 1840.

Linn, John J. *Reminiscences of Fifty Years in Texas.* Austin: Steck Co., 1935.

Lundy, Benjamin. *The Life, Travels, and Opinions of Benjamin Lundy, Including His Journey to Texas and Mexico.* New York: Negro University Press, 1969.

McConnell, H. H. *Five Years a Cavalryman: Or, Sketches of Regular Life on the Texas Frontier, Twenty Odd Years Ago.* Jacksboro: J. N. Rogers & Co., 1899.

McCoy, Joseph G. *Cattle Trade of the West and Southwest.* Ann Arbor: University Microfilms International, 1966.

McIntyre, Benjamin F. *Federals on the Frontier: The Diary of Benjamin F. McIntyre.* Edited by Nannie M. Tilley. Austin: University of Texas Press, 1963.

Maudslay, Robert. *Texas Sheepman: The Reminiscences of Robert Mauds-lay*. Edited by Winifred Kupper. Austin: University of Texas Press, 1951.

Maverick, Samuel. *Samuel Maverick, Texas, 1803–1870: A Collection of Letters, Journals and Memoirs*. Edited by Mary Rowena Maverick Green. San Antonio: Privately printed, 1952.

México. Comisión Pesquisidora de la Frontera del Norte. *Reports of the Committee of Investigation Sent in 1873 by the Mexican Government to the Frontier of Texas*. New York: Baker & Godwin, 1875.

Miller, Susan G. *Sixty Years in the Nueces Valley, 1870–1930*. San Antonio: Naylor Co., 1930.

Mills, Anson. *My Story*. Edited by C. H. Claudy. Washington, D.C.: Published by the author, Press of Byron S. Adams, 1918.

Mills, W. W. *Forty Years at El Paso, 1858–1898*. Introduction by Rex W. Strickland. El Paso: Carl Hertzog, 1962.

Muir, Andrew Forest, ed. *Texas in 1837: An Anonymous Contemporary Narrative*. Austin: University of Texas Press, 1958.

Olmsted, Frederick Law. *A Journey through Texas: Or, A Saddle-Trip on the Southwestern Frontier, with a Statistical Appendix*. New York: Dix, Edwards & Co., 1857. Reprint, Austin: University of Texas Press, 1978.

Page, Frederic Benjamin. *Prairiedom: Rambles and Scrambles in Texas, or, New Estrémadura, by a Suthron*. New York: Paine and Burgess, 1845.

Paine, Albert Bigelow. *Captain Bill McDonald, Texas Ranger: A Story of Frontier Reform*. New York: J. J. Little & Ives Co., 1909.

Parisot, Pierre Fourier, O.M.I. *The Reminiscences of a Texas Missionary*. San Antonio: Johnson Brothers, 1899.

Parker, Amos Andrew. *Trip to the West and Texas* . . . Concord, N.H.: White and Fisher, 1835.

Powers, Stephen. *Afoot and Alone: A Walk from Sea to Sea* . . . Hartford, Conn.: Columbian Book Co., 1894.

Rankin, Melinda. *Twenty Years among the Mexicans: A Narrative of Missionary Labor*. Cincinnati: Central Book Co., 1881.

Rawick, George P., ed. *Texas Narratives*, Parts 1 and 2. Vol. 4 of *The American Slave: A Composite Autobiography*. Westport: Greenwood Publishing Co., 1972.

Reid, John C. *Reid's Tramp: Or, A Journal of the Incidents of Ten Months' Travel* . . . Selma, Ala.: J. Hardy Co., 1858. Reprinted, Austin: Steck Co., 1935.

Remington, Frederic. *Crooked Trails*. Freeport, N.Y.: Books for Libraries Press, 1969.

Richardson, Albert D. *Beyond the Mississippi: From the Great River to the Great Ocean* . . . *1857–1867*. Hartford: American Publishing Co., 1867.

Ringgold, Jennie Parks. *Frontier Days in the Southwest: Pioneer Days in Old Arizona*. San Antonio: Naylor Co., 1952.

Rock, James L., and W. I. Smith. *Southern and Western Texas Guide for 1878*. St. Louis: A. H. Granger, 1878.

Roemer, Ferdinand. *Texas: With Particular Reference to German Immigration and the Physical Appearance of the Country.* Translated by Oswald Mueller. San Antonio: Standard Printing Co., 1935.

Seguín, Juan N. *Personal Memoirs of John N. Seguín: From the Year 1834 to the Retreat of General Woll from the City of San Antonio.* San Antonio: Printed at the Ledger Book and Job Office, 1858.

Sheridan, Philip H. *Personal Memoirs of Philip H. Sheridan, General, United States Army.* 2 vols. New York: C. L. Webster and Co., 1888.

Smith, Ashbel. *Yellow Fever in Galveston, Republic of Texas, 1839: An Account of the Great Epidemic.* Edited by Chauncey D. Leake. Austin: University of Texas Press, 1951.

Smith, E. Kirby. *To Mexico with Scott: Letters of E. Kirby Smith to His Wife.* Edited by Emma Jerome Blackwood. Cambridge: Harvard University Press, 1917.

Smithwick, Noah. *The Evolution of a State.* Austin: Gammel Book Co., 1900.

Solms-Braunfels, Carl of. *Texas, 1844–1845.* Houston: Anson Jones Press, 1936.

Sowell, A. J. *Early Settlers and Indian Fighters of Southwest Texas.* 2 vols. New York: Argosy-Antiquarian Ltd., 1964.

Sterne, Adolphus. *Hurrah For Texas! The Diary of Adolphus Sterne.* Edited by Archie P. McDonald. Waco: Texian Press, 1969.

Sutherland, Mary A. *The Story of Corpus Christi.* Edited by Frank B. Harrison. Houston: Rein & Sons Co., 1916.

Sweet, Alexander E., and John Armoy Knox. *On a Mexican Mustang through Texas: From the Gulf to the Rio Grande.* Hartford: S. S. Scranton & Co., 1883.

———. *Sketches from "Texas Siftings."* New York: Texas Siftings Publishing Co., 1882.

Taylor, Creed. *Tall Men with Long Rifles.* Narrated by James T. De Shields. San Antonio: Naylor Co., 1935.

Taylor, Nathaniel A. *The Coming Empire: Or, Two Thousand Miles in Texas on Horseback.* Houston: N. T. Carlisle, 1877.

Texas (Republic) Convention. *Debates of the Texas Convention, by William F. Weeks, Reporter: Published by Authority of the Convention.* Houston: J. W. Cruger, 1846.

Travis, William Barrett. *The Diary of William Barrett Travis, August 30, 1833–June 26, 1834.* Edited by Robert E. Davis. Waco: Texian Press, 1966.

Vielé, Teresa (Griffin). *"Following the Drum": A Glimpse of Frontier Life.* New York: Rudd & Carleton, 1858.

Walton, W. M. *Life and Adventures of Ben Thompson: The Famous Texan.* Published by the author, 1884. Facsimile edition, Austin: Steck Co., 1956.

Weber, David J., ed. *Northern Mexico on the Eve of the United States Invasion: Rare Imprints Concerning California, Arizona, New Mexico, and Texas.* Facsimile reproductions. New York: Arno Press, 1976.

Williams, R. H. *With the Border Ruffians: Memories of the Far West, 1852–1868.* Edited by E. W. Williams. London: John Murray, 1907.

Winkler, Ernest W., ed. *Manuscript Letters and Documents of Early Texians, 1821–1845.* Austin: Steck Co., 1937.

Woodman, David. *Guide to Texas Emigrants.* Boston: M. Hawes, 1835.

[Wright, John and William?] *Recollections of Western Texas, 1852–1855.* London: W. and F. G. Cash, 1857.

Articles

Benedict, J. W. "Diary of a Campaign against the Comanches." Edited by R. C. Clark. *Southwestern Historical Quarterly* 32 (April 1929): 300–310.

Boom, Aaron M., ed. "Texas in the 1850s, As Viewed by a Recent Arrival." *Southwestern Historical Quarterly* 70 (October 1966): 281–288.

Bostick, Sion R. "Reminiscences of Sion R. Bostick." *Quarterly of the Texas State Historical Association* 5 (October 1901): 85–96.

Bourke, John G. "Notes on the Language and Folk-Usage of the Rio Grande Valley." *Journal of American Folklore* 9 (April–June 1896): 81–116.

Clopper, J. C. "Journal of J. C. Clopper, 1828." *Southwestern Historical Quarterly* 13 (July 1909): 44–80.

Cox, Cornelius C. "From Texas to California in 1849: Diary of C. C. Cox." Edited by Mabelle Eppard Martin. *Southwestern Historical Quarterly* 29 (October 1925): 128–146.

Cuyler, Telamon. "Telamon Cuyler's Diary: To Texas in 1888." Edited by John Hammond Moore. *Southwestern Historical Quarterly* 70 (January 1967): 474–488.

Davis, Ellis Arthur, ed. *The Historical Encyclopedia of Texas.* 2 vols. Austin: Texas Historical Society, n.d.

Davis, Richard Harding. "Our Troops on the Border." *Harper's Weekly*, March 26, 1892, p. 294.

Eve, Joseph. "A Letter Book of Joseph Eve, United States Chargé d'Affaires to Texas." Edited by Joseph M. Nance. *Southwestern Historical Quarterly* 43 (October 1939): 196–221; (April 1940): 486–510.

Gaines, John Pollard. "Diary of Major John Pollard Gaines of Kentucky, Volunteer Cavalry." Edited by Dorman H. Winfrey. *Texana* 1 (Winter 1963): 30–37.

Gardiner, Charles A. "The Future of the Negro." *North American Review* 139 (July 1884): 78–99.

Harby, Lee C. "Texan Types and Contrast." *Harper's New Monthly Magazine* 81 (July 1890): 229–246.

Johnston, Eliza. "The Diary of Eliza (Mrs. Albert Sidney) Johnston." Edited by Charles P. Roland and Richard C. Robbins. *Southwestern Historical Quarterly* 60 (April 1957): 463–500.

"The Latin Races in America." *Southern Review* 9 (April 1871): 320–346.

McClintock, William A. "Journal of a Trip through Texas and Northern Mexico in 1846–1847." *Southwestern Historical Quarterly* 34 (October 1930): 141–158.

Myer, Albert J. "I Am Already Quite a Texan: Albert J. Myer's Letters from Texas, 1854–1856." Edited by David A. Clary. *Southwestern Historical Quarterly* 82 (July 1978):25–76.

Smyth, George W. "The Autobiography of George W. Smyth," edited by Winnie Allen. *Southwestern Historical Quarterly* 36 (January 1933): 200–214.

Speed, Jonathan Gilmer. "The Hunt for Garza." *Harper's Weekly*, January 30, 1892, pp. 103–104.

Spofford, Harriet. "San Antonio de Béxar." *Harper's New Monthly Magazine* 55 (November 1877):831–850.

Taylor, Frank H. "Through Texas." *Harper's New Monthly Magazine* 59 (October 1879):712–713.

SECONDARY SOURCES

Books

Barker, Eugene C. *The Life of Stephen F. Austin, Founder of Texas, 1793–1836*. Nashville and Dallas: Cokesburg Press, 1925.

Barrera, Mario. *Race and Class in the Southwest: A Theory of Racial Inequality*. Notre Dame: University of Notre Dame Press, 1979.

Bedichek, Roy. *Adventures with a Texas Naturalist*. Austin: University of Texas Press, 1961.

Berkhofer, Robert F., Jr. *The White Man's Indian: Images of the American Indian from Columbus to the Present*. New York: Alfred A. Knopf, 1978.

Bertelson, David. *The Lazy South*. New York: Oxford University Press, 1967.

Brown, Richard Maxwell. *Strains of Violence: Historical Studies of American Violence and Vigilantism*. New York: Oxford University Press, 1975.

Canales, José T. *Juan N. Cortina Presents His Motion for a New Trial*. San Antonio: Artes Gráficas, 1951.

Cardoso, Lawrence. *Mexican Emigration to the United States, 1897–1931*. Tucson: University of Arizona Press, 1980.

Carter, Thomas R. *Mexican-Americans in School: A History of Educational Neglect*. Princeton: College Entrance Examination Board, 1970.

Castillo, Pedro, and Albert Camarillo, eds. *Furia y muerte: Los bandidos chicanos*. Los Angeles: Aztlán Publications, 1973.

Chabot, Frederick Charles. *With the Makers of San Antonio: Genealogies of the Early Latin, Anglo-American, and German Families* . . . San Antonio: Privately published, printing by Artes Gráficas, 1937.

Connor, Seymour V. *Texas: A History*. New York: Thomas Y. Crowell Co., 1971.

Corning, Leavitt. *Baronial Forts of the Big Bend*. San Antonio: Trinity University Press, 1967.

Davis, David Brion. *The Problem of Slavery in Western Culture*. Ithaca: Cornell University Press, 1966.

De León, Arnoldo. *In re Ricardo Rodríguez: An Attempt at Chicano Disfranchisement in San Antonio, 1896–1897.* San Antonio: Caravel Press,
————. *The Tejano Community, 1836–1900.* Albuquerque: University of New Mexico Press, 1982.

Diamond Jubilee, 1847–1922, of the Diocese of Galveston and St. Mary's Cathedral. Compiled by the priests of the seminary. Galveston: Knapp Bros., Printers, 1922.

Drinnon, Richard. *Facing West: The Metaphysics of Indian Hunting and Empire Building.* Minneapolis: University of Minnesota Press, 1980.

Fenley, Florence. *Old Times: Their Own Stories.* Uvalde, Tex.: Hornby Press, 1939.

Foley, Douglas E., et al. *From Peones to Politicos: Ethnic Relations in a South Texas Town, 1900 to 1977.* Austin: Center for Mexican American Studies, University of Texas, 1977.

Frederickson, George M. *White Supremacy: A Comparative Study in American and South African History.* Oxford: Oxford University Press, 1981.

García, Juan Ramón. *Operation Wetback: The Mass Deportation of Mexican Undocumented Workers in 1954.* Westport, Conn.: Greenwood Press, 1980.

García, Mario T. *Desert Immigrants: The Mexicans of El Paso, 1880–1920.* New Haven: Yale University Press, 1981.

Goldfinch, Charles W. *Juan Cortina, 1824–1892: A Re-appraisal.* Brownsville: Bishop's Print Shop, 1950.

Gossett, Thomas F. *Race: The History of an Idea in America.* Dallas: Southern Methodist University Press, 1963.

Grebler, Leo, Joan W. Moore, and Ralph Guzmán. *The Mexican American People: The Nation's Second Largest Minority.* New York: Free Press, 1970.

Grimes, Roy, ed. *300 Years in Victoria County.* Victoria, Tex.: Victoria Advocate Publishing Co., 1968.

Hatcher, Mattie Alice. *The Opening of Texas to Foreign Settlement, 1801–1821.* Austin: University of Texas Press, 1927.

Hobsbawm, J. *Primitive Rebels: Studies in Archaic Forms of Social Movements in the Nineteenth and Twentieth Centuries.* New York: W. W. Norton & Co., 1965.

Hoffman, Abraham. *Unwanted Mexican Americans in the Great Depression: Repatriation Pressures, 1929–1939.* Tucson: University of Arizona Press, 1974.

Hollon, W. Eugene. *Beyond the Cross Timbers: The Travels of Randolph P. Marcy, 1812–1887.* Norman: University of Oklahoma Press, 1955.

Horsman, Reginald. *Race and Manifest Destiny: The Origins of American Racial Anglo-Saxonism.* Cambridge: Harvard University Press, 1981.

Hunter, J. Marvin. *The Trail Drives of Texas.* 2 vols. New York: Argosy-Antiquarian Ltd., 1963.

Huson, Hobart. *Refugio: A Comprehensive History.* 2 vols. Woodsboro: Rooke Foundation, Inc., 1953.

Jordan, Winthrop D. *White over Black: American Attitudes toward the Negro, 1550–1812.* Chapel Hill: University of North Carolina Press,

Kibbe, Pauline. *The Latin Americans of Texas.* Albuquerque: University of New Mexico Press, 1946.

Kovel, Joel. *White Racism: A Psychohistory.* New York: Vintage Books, 1970.

Lathrop, Barnes F. *Migration into East Texas, 1835–1860: A Study from the United States Census.* Austin: State Historical Association, 1949.

Lewis, Lloyd. *Captain Sam Grant.* Boston: Little, Brown and Co., 1950.

Lowrie, Samuel H. *Culture Conflict in Texas, 1821–1836.* New York: AMS Press, 1967.

McGrath, Sister Paul of the Cross. *Political Nativism in Texas, 1825–1860.* Washington: Catholic University of America, 1930.

Madsen, William. *Mexican Americans of South Texas.* 2d ed. New York: Holt, Rinehart and Winston, 1973.

Meier, Matt, and Feliciano Rivera, eds. *Readings on La Raza: The Twentieth Century.* New York: Hill and Wang, 1974.

Mirandé, Alfredo, and Evangelina Enríquez. *La Chicana: The Mexican American Woman.* Chicago: University of Chicago Press, 1979.

Montejano, David. *Race, Labor Repression, and Capitalist Agriculture: Notes from South Texas, 1920–1930.* Berkeley: Institute for the Study of Social Change, 1977.

Morales, Armando. *Ando sangrando! I Am Bleeding.* La Puente, Calif.: Perspectiva Publications, 1972.

Nance, Joseph Milton. *Attack and Counter-Attack: The Texas-Mexican Frontier, 1842.* Austin: University of Texas Press, 1964.

Nash, Gary B. *Red, White, and Black: The Peoples of Early America.* 2d ed. Englewood Cliffs, N.J.: Prentice-Hall, 1982.

Paredes, Américo. *"With His Pistol in His Hand": A Border Ballad and Its Hero.* Austin: University of Texas Press, 1958.

Perales, Alonso. *Are We Good Neighbors?* San Antonio: Artes Gráficas, 1948.

Pierce, Frank C. *A Brief History of the Lower Rio Grande Valley.* Menasha, Wis.: George Banta Publishing Co., 1917.

Pitt, Leonard. *The Decline of the Californios: A Social History of the Spanish-Speaking Californians, 1846–1890.* Berkeley: University of California Press, 1970.

Raht, Carlysle Graham. *The Romance of Davis Mountains and Big Bend Country.* El Paso: Raht Books Co., 1919.

Richardson, Rupert, Ernest Wallace, and Adrian Anderson. *Texas: The Lone Star State.* 3d ed. Englewood Cliffs, N.J.: Prentice-Hall, 1970.

Robinson, Cecil. *Mexico and the Hispanic Southwest in American Literature.* (Revised from *With the Ears of Strangers: The Mexican in American Literature.*) Tucson: University of Arizona Press, 1977.

Rosenbaum, Robert J. *Mexicano Resistance in the Southwest: "The Sacred*

Right of Self-Preservation." Austin: University of Texas Press, 1981.

Samora, Julian, Joe Bernal, and Albert Peña. *Gunpowder Justice: A Reassessment of the Texas Rangers.* Notre Dame: University of Notre Dame

Sanders, Ronald. *Lost Tribes and Promised Lands: The Origins of American Racism.* Boston: Little, Brown and Co., 1978.

Schwartz, Rosalie. *Across the River to Freedom: U.S. Negroes in Mexico.* El Paso: Texas Western Press, 1975.

Sheehan, Bernard W. *Savagism and Civility: Indians and Englishmen in Colonial Virginia.* Cambridge: Cambridge University Press, 1980.

Slotkin, Richard. *Regeneration through Violence: The Mythology of the American Frontier, 1600–1860.* Middletown, Conn.: Wesleyan University Press, 1973.

Sonnichson, C. L. *Ten Texas Feuds.* Albuquerque: University of New Mexico Press, 1957.

Takaki, Ronald T. *Iron Cages: Race and Culture in Nineteenth Century America.* New York: Knopf, 1979.

Taylor, Paul S. *An American Mexican Frontier: Nueces County, Texas.* Chapel Hill: University of North Carolina Press, 1934.

Thompson, Jerry Don. *Vaqueros in Blue and Gray.* Austin: Presidial Press, 1976.

Tijerina, Andrés A. *The History of Mexican Americans in Lubbock County.* Lubbock: Texas Tech Press, 1979.

A Twentieth Century History of Southwest Texas. 2 vols. Chicago: Lewis Publishing Co., 1907.

Webb, Walter Prescott. *The Texas Rangers: A Century of Frontier Defense.* Boston: Houghton Mifflin Co., 1935.

Weber, David, ed. *Foreigners in Their Native Land.* Albuquerque: University of New Mexico Press, 1973.

Woodman, Lyman. *Cortina: Rogue of the Rio Grande.* San Antonio: Naylor Press, 1950.

Articles

Bean, Frank D., and Benjamin S. Bradshaw. "An Exploratory Study of Intermarriage between Mexican Americans and Anglo Americans, 1850–1960." *Southwestern Sociological Association Proceedings* 1970: 120–125.

———. "Intermarriage between Persons of Spanish and Non-Spanish Surname: Changes from the Mid-Nineteenth to the Mid-Twentieth Century." *Social Science Quarterly* 51 (September 1970): 389–394.

Dysart, Jane. "Mexican Women in San Antonio, 1850–1860: The Assimilation Process." *Western Historical Quarterly* 7 (October 1976): 365–375.

Elliot, Claude. "Union Sentiment in Texas, 1861–1865." *Southwestern Historical Quarterly* 50 (April 1947): 449–477.

Gutman, Herbert G. "Work, Culture, and Society in Industrializing America," in *Work, Culture, and Society in Industrializing America: Essays* in *American Working Class History*, edited by Herbert G. Gutman. New York: Knopf, 1976.

Hager, William M. "The Nueces Town Raid of 1875: A Border Incident." *Arizona and the West* 1 (Spring 1959):258–270.

Jordan, Terry G. "Population Origins in Texas, 1850." *Geographical Review* 59 (January 1969):83–103.

Lack, Paul D. "Slavery and Vigilantism in Austin, Texas, 1840–1860." *Southwestern Historical Quarterly* 85 (July 1981):1–20.

Langum, David J. "Californios and the Image of Indolence." *Western Historical Quarterly* 9 (April 1978):181–196.

Limón, José. "El Primer Congreso Mexicanista de 1911: A Precursor to Contemporary Chicanismo." *Aztlán: Chicano Journal of the Social Sciences and the Arts* 5 (Spring and Fall 1974):85–118.

McLemore, S. Dale. "The Origins of Mexican American Subordination in Texas." *Social Science Quarterly* 53 (March 1973):656–671.

Morgan, Edmund S. "The Labor Problem at Jamestown, 1602–1618." *American Historical Review* 76 (June 1971):595–611.

Padilla, Ray V. "A Critique of Pittian History." *El Grito* 6 (Fall 1972):3–44.

Paredes, Américo. "On 'Gringo,' 'Greaser,' and Other Neighborly Names." In *Singers and Storytellers*, edited by Mody C. Boatright et al. Dallas: Southern Methodist University Press, 1961.

Paredes, Raymund. "The Mexican Image in American Travel Literature." *New Mexico Historical Review* 52 (January 1977):5–29.

———. "The Origins of Anti-Mexican Sentiment in the United States." In *New Directions in Chicano Scholarship*, edited by Ricardo Romo and Raymund Paredes, pp. 139–166. La Jolla: University of California at San Diego, 1978.

Pierce, Gerald. "The Great Wolf Hunt: Tennessee Volunteers in Texas." *West Tennessee Historical Society Papers* 19 (1965):5–20.

Slotkin, Richard S. Review of Ronald Sanders' *Lost Tribes and Promised Lands*. *New Republic*, May 6, 1978, pp. 25–28.

Smyrl, Frank H. "Texans in the Union Army, 1861–1865." *Southwestern Historical Quarterly* 65 (October 1961):234–250.

Surace, Samuel J. "Achievement, Discrimination, and Mexican Americans." *Comparative Studies in Society and History* 24 (April 1982):315–339.

Tjarks, Alicia V. "Comparative Demographic Analysis of Texas, 1777–1793." *Southwestern Historical Quarterly* 77 (January 1974):291–338.

Tyler, Ronnie C. "Fugitive Slaves in Mexico." *Journal of Negro History* 57 (January 1972):1–12.

Vaca, Nick. "The Mexican American in the Social Sciences." *El Grito: A Journal of Contemporary Mexican American Thought* 3 (Spring 1970):3–24; 4 (Fall 1970):17–51.

Weber, David J. "Here Rests Juan Espinosa: Toward a Clearer Look at the Image of the 'Indolent' Californios." *Western Historical Quarterly* 10 (January 1979):61–68.

————. "'Scarce More than Apes': Historical Roots of Anglo-American Stereotypes of Mexicans in the Border Region." In *New Spain's Far Northern Frontier: Essays on Spain in the American West, 1540–1821,* edited by David J. Weber, pp. 295–307. Albuquerque: University of New Mexico Press, 1979.

Wilcox, Seb S. "The Laredo City Election and Riot of April, 1886." *Southwestern Historical Quarterly* 45 (July 1941): 1–23.

Theses and Dissertations

Benavides, Ilma M. "General Adrian Woll's Invasion of San Antonio in 1842." M.A. thesis, University of Texas, 1952.

Crews, James Robert. "Reconstruction in Brownsville, Texas." M.A. thesis, Texas Tech University, 1969.

Crisp, James Ernest. "Anglo-Texan Attitudes toward the Mexican, 1821–1845." Ph.D. dissertation, Yale University, 1976.

Crook, Carland Elaine. "San Antonio, Texas, 1846–1861." M.A. thesis, Rice University, 1964.

Downs, Fane. "The History of Mexicans in Texas, 1820–1845." Ph.D. dissertation, Texas Tech University, 1970.

Evans, James Leroy. "The Indian Savage, the Mexican Bandit, the Chinese Heathen—Three Popular Stereotypes." Ph.D. dissertation, University of Texas at Austin, 1967.

González, Jovita. "Social Life in Cameron, Starr, and Zapata Counties." M.A. thesis, University of Texas at Austin, 1930.

O'Neal, John William. "Texas, 1791–1835: A Study in Manifest Destiny." M.A. thesis, East Texas State University, 1969.

Paredes, Raymund. "The Image of the Mexican in American Literature." Ph.D. dissertation, University of California, Berkeley, 1974.

Tijerina, Andrew Anthony. "Tejanos and Texas: The Native Mexicans of Texas, 1820–1850." Ph.D. dissertation, University of Texas at Austin, 1977.

White, William Wilson. "Migration into West Texas, 1845–1860." M.A. thesis, University of Texas, 1948.

Index